T0209740

A Christian Theology

ON MAN'S NEED OF REDEMPTION, GOD'S REDEMPTIVE PURPOSE, AND CHRIST'S REDEMPTIVE WORK

Dr. John Thomas Wylie

authorHOUSE®

AuthorHouse™
1663 Liberty Drive
Bloomington, IN 47403
www.authorhouse.com
Phone: 1 (800) 839-8640

Published by AuthorHouse 09/03/2019

ISBN: 978-1-7283-2622-1 (sc)
ISBN: 978-1-7283-2621-4 (e)

Print information available on the last page.

Any people depicted in stock imagery provided by Getty Images are models,
and such images are being used for illustrative purposes only.
Certain stock imagery © Getty Images.

This book is printed on acid-free paper.

Scripture quotations marked KJV are from the Holy Bible, King James Version
(Authorized Version). First published in 1611. Quoted from the KJV Classic
Reference Bible, Copyright © 1983 by The Zondervan Corporation.

The Holy Bible (1982) New Interpreter's Version. Grand Rapids, MI.: Thomas Nelson
Inc. (Used By Permission)

The New Testament In The Language of The People (1937, 1949) Chicago, Ill.:
Charles B Williams, Bruce Humphries, Inc. Moody Bible Institute (Used By
Permission)

Contents

CHAPTER THREE

CHAPTER FOUR

CHAPTER FIVE

Introduction

Man's Need Of Redemption From Sin

IN THIS PUBLICATION, TREATING the Christian Doctrine of Salvation, ends up important to make them comprehend the nature and ruin of transgression (sin). Christ came to look for and to save the individuals who were lost in sin. We have to value the awfulness of that from which he saves us.

This isn't to be interpreted as meaning that salvation is only liberation from something. It is sure in its tendency. Salvation incorporates every one of the riches of the blessings engaged with the life of fellowship with God into which he brings us by his grace. Truth be told, we are not really saved from sin aside from as the life of transgression is dislodged by an actual existence of fellowship with God.

What Is Sin?

A BASIC DEFINITION IS "transgression of the law" (I John 3:4). Sin might be seen as a solitary demonstration of transgressing or it might be seen as a state in which all men are or have been (Rom. 3:23; I John 1:8). The results of sin are physical death (Gen. 2:17; Rom. 5:12).

The wages of Sin, under the age of the reign of Christ, is spiritual death (Rom. 6:23). The seat of all is the heart (Matt. 15:19), in light of the fact that out of it come everything one says or does. Since man was in sin, God loved man and sent Jesus to save men from sin (John 3:16; Acts 10:43).

The unpardonable sin is by all accounts the denial of the power of God which is invested in Jesus Christ (Matt. 12:31).

What Is Redemption?

THIS MEANS THE LOOSING of somebody by the paying of a price. It is utilized to express God's work in the salvation of man. In the Old Testament the people were redeemed through the firstborn for five shekels (Num. 18:16). In the New Testament Jesus Christ is compared with a Savior supernaturally sent. He uncovers or reveals the love of God for his people (Rom. 3:24; Gal. 3:13; Eph. 1:7; I Pet. 1:18; I Cor. 1:30). This redemption of man implies that man was under bondage to sin (Gal. 3:13; I Cor. 15:56) and the power of Satan and death (Acts 26:18; Heb. 2:14,15).

Jesus Christ, in his death, redeemed us from the scourge or the bondage of sin. Also, presently, as followers of Christ, we can look for the redemption of the body (Heb. 2:9; Acts 3:19; II Tim. 2:26; I Cor. 15:55-57).

Reverend Dr. John Thomas Wylie

Chapter ONE

Sin As Against God

WE MAY STATE THAT sin is against the state. Unethical (immoral) behavior is against society. However, "sin" is against God. In a goddess world sin would have no importance. As man lose the cognizance of God the sense of sin likewise leaves their minds and hearts.

Then again, as the vision of God is restored in an individual or a general public of individuals, he (or they) will be stricken with a feeling of transgression (sin).

The Old Testament focuses on God and his movement on the earth. The scholars of the Old Testament see man and the world in connection to God and his dealings with man.

We would, in this way, hope to discover much in their compositions concerning sin. Furthermore, that is our specialty find. There are a striking number and assortment of words in the Old Testament (just as in the New Testament) dealing with sin. It will be appeared as follows, in any case, that the fullest exposure of sin and its temperament comes just in connection to the last disclosure of God in Christ.

What we have quite recently said does not imply that sin against the state, or an unethical life, isn't sin. It implies rather that these are sin just by prudence of the way that the state and the human social order are periods of the perfect order of the world.

Both the state and human society are appointed of God. They are fractional articulations of the will of God. So far as these are articulations of the will of God, at that point, sin against the state or an infringement of the will of God as communicated in human society is sin. Sin would have no importance in a goddess world.

This does not mean that a man must be specifically aware of God to submit sin. By and large the miscreant isn't straightforwardly aware of God. It is the absence of an awareness of God (maybe inferring a rejection of God) that is the focal thing in man's condition of sin. The specific heart of sin is the putting of God out of man's mind and life.

Dr. John Thomas Wylie

Temptation As Related To Sin

SIN COMES AS THE result and consequence of temptation. Temptation is an induction or incitement to sin. Temptation can barely be said to be the reason for transgression (sin); it is somewhat that event. Sin maybe would not be without temptation, but rather the reason for sin is the "will of man".

However to talk about a reason for sin might be excessively mechanical. It may be smarter to talk about it as far as "moral choice" and "good duty." Causality sounds excessively like one block in succession thumping others over. Moral duty (or moral choice) lies in man's will.

Temptation impacts the will, however it doesn't decide it. The will is self-deciding. Else it isn't will; aside from the power of self-determination it would be a mechanical power, not personal will.

All through the Bible temptation is an instigation to sin originating from without. It is along these lines conceivable in light of the fact that man is certifiably not an independent being. He is a limited creature. He is social in his tendency and can exist just in relation to other beings and powers. Evil in the Bible is viewed as a framework with the devil as its head.

Numerous individuals today deny that there is any devil. They hold that this thought of a personal devil is perspective or scientific view of the world. But, the inquiry concerning whether there is a personal devil or not will be not one that legitimately comes surprisingly close to logical examination.

What's more, with regards to the heading of theory on the inquiry, the main rule that would essentially avoid a personal devil is the rule that would deny all close to home organization on the earth and decrease the universe out and out to an arrangement of generic powers. Be that as it may, this would not just prohibit a personal devil; it would likewise reject God as an individual and man as well. Such a view is intolerable in religion.

The thought is some of the time propelled that to ascribe sin to the office of the devil is to decrease man's awareness of other expectations for sin. In any case, this is a mixed up idea. This is appeared by the way that it didn't have this impact with the scriptural writers.

No authors have ever indicated such an infiltrating feeling of the blame and power of sin, but in the meantime they viewed sin as being because of satanic temptation. A similar thing is true with reference to Christians who believe in Satan.

Rather than reducing their feeling of the dreadfulness and ruin of sin, it has rather been expanded. Such a man as Martin Luther is a genuine precedent. Then again, there is valid justification to address at any rate if a skepticism in a personal devil does not have a chosen propensity to make men see sin as a light thing.

It isn't against this view the possibility of a devil and evil spirits is to be found in different religions. The possibility of a divine being (a god) is to be found in other religions. Be that as it may, we don't reject the thought for that reason. The agency of a powerful personal evil spirit would clarify the power and diligence of sin in human life. It is said that the possibility of a personal devil is to attribute to the spontaneous inclination of the mind to trait wonders the reason for which isn't comprehended to personal agency of some likeness thereof.

This may be allowed. The inquiry isn't whether the conviction is to be ascribed to such a psychological tendency, but whether it drives us toward truth or not. On other inquiries, for example, the presence of God and the immortality of the soul, we for the most part say that a natural tendency of the mind, prompting for all intents and purposes a universal belief, is to be trusted. In any event this would not be against the belief in a personal devil.

There are at least like two things that support the view that there is an personal devil. One is the presence, power, and steadiness of moral persistence evil in this world. That sin and sinners exist, nobody with the least good observation can deny.

Be that as it may, it isn't only an issue of accounting for sin and sinners, it is additionally an issue of accounting the power and persistence of sin, for what is by all accounts seem to be a kingdom of evil.

In the second place, that there is such a kingdom of underhandedness, of evil under Satan as the head is the view exhibited in the Bible. What we demand here is that there are sure marvels which can best be accounted for on the hypothesis that such a evil personality exists and works in human life to advance sin, destroy man, and thwart the purposes of God.

The origin of Satan is an inquiry on which next to zero light is tossed in the Bible. There are two things that we can avow with a reasonable level of certainty on general grounds, not by specific Scripture teaching.

One is that Satan is a created being. We can confirm this for two reasons. One is that the Scriptures teach that God made all things both visible and invisible (Col. 1:16). The other reason is that in the idea of the case there can be only one eternal and uncreated being. God is simply the self-existent being. The other thing we feel certain of is that God did not make Satan a evil being. God presumably made him, but did not make him a fallen angel (devil).

Satan certainly made himself a devil by rebellion against God and after that by offering himself to the work of luring others to sin. Be that as it may, about how and when this occurred we have no light.

Since the times of Milton, or before, the view has been predominant that Satan was the head of the fallen angels. However, for this view there is no particular Scripture authority. It might be true or it may not. Sacred Scripture writing can't be claimed for it.

The Bible at that point, gives us no record of the birthplace of sin known to mankind. It gives just the birthplace of sin among men. It follows the root of root among men to evil enticement.

Usually accepted that temptation can claim only to that which is evil in man, to that which is degraded and corrupted. Be that as it may, this is false, untrue. The temptation of Eve, just as the temptation of Jesus, makes this obvious. Look at the temptation of Eve with reference to this point.

In Genesis 3:6 it is clarified that the forbidden fruit spoke to three desires on Eve's part, all of which is an ordinary desire. The first was the physical hunger or the craving for food. Eve saw that the tree was useful for food. It looked good to eat. Undoubtedly it isn't ethically (morally) wrong to be ravenous or to want nourishment.

To eat maybe inside itself an morally apathetic act. Customarily, in any event, it is right. It was to this consummately regular and typical desire for sustenance (food) that the devil advanced in tempting Eve and furthermore on tempting Jesus.

At that point it is said that Eve saw that the tree was a pleasure to the eyes. It spoke to the sense of the beautiful. What's more, to want the delightful is unquestionably not wrong inside itself. At that point it is said that she saw that the tree was to be desire to make one wise. It engaged the craving for learning (knowledge). This again is a longing that is ordinarily right.

So the devil tempted Eve by speaking to these three desires that are typical in any individual. Wherein, at that point, comprised her sin? In attempting to fulfill these typical desires of her being in this wrong way, in opposition to the will of God.

This encourages us to see how temptation makes its intrigue to desires of our tendency which, whenever fulfilled in the correct way, are altogether typical and right. It is a mixed up thought that temptation must interest the base. It might engage what is most elevated and best. Sin is the depravity of the great and the most exceedingly sin might be the corruption or perversion of the best.

Calvin said that nothing known to man is "evil in nature; since neither the evil and fiendishness of men and villains, nor the sins which continue from that source are from mere nature but from a corruption of nature." Not the use, but the maltreatment, the abuse of God's world causes trouble. This helps to correct another false impression with references to sin.

We here and there believe that the higher one goes in the good and spiritual life less subject to temptation he will be. This isn't true, as each Christian realizes who has gained any ground in spiritual issues and as the case of the Savior himself shows.

It would be closer to the truth to state that the higher one goes in the spiritual life the subtler and more grounded does temptation move toward becoming. It additionally causes us to see how the most exceedingly worst sins are the depravity of the highest and holiest relations throughout everyday life. Sin dependably shows up in the pretense of a good. Else it would be no temptation.

The epistle of James discloses to us that a man is enticed when he is drawn away and lured by his own desire (1:14). The creator says that lust produces sin, and sin death.

This does not intend to preclude temptation from outside from claiming man. It is depicting the psychological course of sin and death. The thing mulled over is definitely not a temptation except if desired. Unless there is an intrigue to man's desire, temptation would be lacking.

James also reveals to us that God can't be tempted and that he doesn't tempt man (1:13). God can't be tempted in light of the fact that his goodness and wisdom are absolute. He doesn't tempt man for the same reason. As absolutely good he is the source of all good and of nothing that is morally evil.

However we find in the Bible that God tries men. He tests or tries men that he may create and affirm them in goodness. The devil tempts men that he may destroy them. A same event in a man's life might be from God's stance a testing to build up the man, and from the devil's perspective a temptation to destroy him.

The Nature Of Sin Due To Bodily Appetites And Instincts

1. SIN IS BECAUSE of man's ownership of a body. This connects sin with man's physical living being (a physical organism). In its extraordinary form it depends on the hypothesis that issue is basically evil. Henceforth man is a sinner by prudence of his ownership of a body. It increases some credibility from the utilization of the expression

"flesh" in the Bible to indicate man as frail and mortal, and, in any event in Paul, as "sinful."

However, while the expression "flesh" denotes man as weak and mortal, and keeping in mind that Paul utilizes the term to mean the circle of the activity of the sin principle, still the biblical authors never view the body as being evil within itself.

This thought came into Christian religious theology from Greek philosophy. It was strengthened by the doctrine of original sin, particularly in the extreme form in which it was held by Augustine. This prompted the possibility that everything natural were evil.

The natural instincts and propensities of the body were evil and ought to be suppressed. A devout life and an enthusiastic body could scarcely go together. Thus, the possibility that to cultivate a life of devotion one must pull back from the world and subdue one's body with all its natural desires and propensities.

This view has in later times taken on a somewhat modified form due to the theory of evolutioin. This hypothesis has prompted the propensity to see sin as the remaining parts of animal instinct in man. Sin, thusly, isn't so much a thing that is culpable as it is certain animal tendencies that must be curbed and brought under the control of man's rational will. There was no fall of man as per this theory.

Neither form of this theory is an adequate record of sin. The body is never viewed as evil in the Scriptures. Paul does not mean by the expression "flesh," when used as an equivalent word for the sin principle, the body. He doesn't see the body as sinful in itself.

He talks about the mind of thoughts of the flesh (Rom. 8:6,7). What's more, he incorporates envy, strife, jealousy, and so forth, as works of the flesh, which demonstrates that the flesh was a spiritual and not only a bodily principle (Gal. 5:19-21).

Sin can't be viewed simply as the remains of animal instinct in man. However, most malevolent factor in sin is associated principally with the bodily organism and physical desires or instincts, but the most diabolical factor in sin is not connected primarily with the animal appetites or instincts of man. Such sins as pride and ambition can hardly be viewed as the remains of animal instincts.

Jesus denounced most seriously, not the persons who were liable of what we call sins of the flesh, for example, intoxication, and extramarital perversion, but those who were guilty of self-righteous pride and hypocrisy.

Sin As Weakness and Limitation

———————

2. ANOTHER THEORY WITH regards to the idea of transgression (sin) can be summed up in the statement: Sin is limitation because of man's finiteness. It isn't deliberate and willful transgression; it is shortcoming, weakness and error. This theory goes back in various structures in any event to the extent of Socrates.

Socrates instructed that no man would intentionally do what he knew would hurt himself; that man fouls up in light of the fact that he doesn't know better. Sin, in this manner, isn't willful. Theodore Parker is a delegate of this view among early New England Unitarians.

Parker said that, sin bears the same relation to man's developing spiritual life that falling does to a youngster's figuring out how to walk. The youngster can't figure out how to walk without falling. Be that as it may, by falling the child figures out how to walk. So by his moral botching man learns the lessons necessary to the development of his moral and spiritual life.

This view takes the components of willfulness and guilt out of sin. In any case, the Scriptures state that these components are there, as still, conscience affirms likewise - especially an enlightened Christian conscience.

Socrates and Paul held inverse rationalities (opposite philosophies) with reference to the issue. Socrates said in substance: "What man needs is knowledge concerning what is right and what's wrong; and when he knows the right, he will do it."

Paul said in actuality; "When a man recognizes what is right, he won't do it since he cannot. He doesn't have the moral ability. There is in him a principle of sin that is too strong for him.

What man needs isn't just a knowledge of what is right, but some motive power to empower him to do the right. Without this power he is defenseless (helpless). Parker's view that man figures out how to do right by fouling up won't bear the trial of experience. Experience shows that pretty much all man learns by sinning is to sin.

The facts demonstrate that man couldn't be tempted and henceforth couldn't sin unless man were finite. God can't be tempted on the grounds that he is infinite in wisdom and power.

Man's finite, his creatureliness, makes him subject to temptation, and henceforth to sin. In any case, it isn't true that his creatureliness within itself establishes sin.

Besides, there is a moral shortcoming (weakness) that grows out of sin. Sinning produces a condition of sin that definitely prompts further sinning. Sin is in excess of an oversight, a mistake or bumble. As officially noticed, this is the blunder in the view that man figures out how to walk morally by falling. Falling does not create strength to walk; it just motivations shortcoming (more weakness, sin) of character that prompts further falling.

Rebellion Against God

ASSUME WE TAKE A tentative meaning of sin the definition that sin is "rebellion against the will of God." To clarify the idea of sin as rebellion against God, the accompanying focuses require emphasis:

The Element of Willfulness In Sin

ONE FACTOR AS A part of man's personality, one thing that marks him as a being created in the divine image, is the power of will. To be equipped for obedience or disobedience, man must have the power of will.

To be capable of obedience or disobedience, man must have the power of choice. Obedience to the law of their being merits no acclaim in light of the fact that these must choose between limited options. With them it involves physical need or creature impulse. Their adjustment to the law of their being is obedience only in a secondary sense. Man obeys in light of the fact that he wills to obey.

As allowed to obey or disobey, man gets commands from God. For what reason was man singled out toward the start as the one being whom God had made to whom God should address a particular command, except if it be that man by virtue of his personality has the power of obedience or disobedience?

This principle as a presupposition underlies every one of God's dealings with man as recorded in the Bible. Man is more than a mechanism; he is a person. Indeed, even God his Creator respects his personality.

This turns out much more obviously in the way that God commands man, as well as entreats, persuades, exhorts him. God's regard for man's will turn out in the way that God utilizes men as his messengers to convince their colleagues to obey God.

A standout amongst the most impressive things about the scriptural revelation of God is the infinite patience of God in dealing with erring and sinful man. God was never without his witnesses, and after he had gone into covenant relations with Israel as a country, the record is one long story of the falling away from the faith and unfaithfulness of Israel and of the faithfulness and longsuffering of Jehovah.

This turns out through the entire of Old Testament history and is the subject of such songs as the seventy-eighth.

his principle is stunningly brought out likewise in the life and teachings of Jesus. Jesus sobs over Jerusalem as he see the looming fate of the city. He gives as the explanation behind its coming devastation that its occupants would not be gathered to him (Luke 13:34).

This comes out no where more plainly than in Paul's extraordinary saying in II Corinthians 5:19,20. He says God is in Christ reconciling the world unto himself. At that point he includes: "We are ambassadors therefore on behalf of Christ, as though God were entreating by us; we beseech you for Christ, be ye reconciled to God."

It's anything but an surprising thing that God the Creator should command man his creature. It shows particularly the respect that God has for man's will and the element of willfulness in man's rebellion against God.

Sin And Knowledge

2. IF MAN'S SIN is willful, it must be sin against light. Where there is no knowledge of moral truth, there can be no sin in the full sense of the term. Maybe this is suggested in Paul's explanation that where there is no law, neither is there transgression (Rom. 4:15).

He likewise says that through the law is the knowledge of sin (Rom. 3:20). In Romans 7 Paul depicts a state in which he says that at one time he was alive without the law. In any case, when the commandment came, "sin revived, and I passed on."

When he came to realize a specific thing as forbidden of the law, he didn't subsequently avoid doing that thing, but instead came to do it. This demonstrates there was sin intimate connection between a knowledge of the will of God and sin as a functioning principle in human life. (Peruse vv. 7-11).

In any case, knowledge of moral and spiritual things, especially knowledge of God and his will, assume disclosure on God's part. In actuality, we consider sin in the Bible personally identified with two other thoughts - disclosure on God's part and a knowledge of that disclosure on man's part.

All in all, there are four phases in this revelation, all associated with sin in the New Testament. The first is the revelation of God in nature or the physical world. This, Paul examines in Romans 1:18 ff. The invisible things of God are plainly observed, being seen through the things that are made, even his everlasting power and divinity.

Paul says that this knowledge of God that comes through nature leaves men without excuse. In spite of the fact that men knew God as hence uncovered (revealed), they would not respect him and serve him. As an outcome they wound up blinded. They were dove into excessive idolatry and a wide range of moral and spiritual degradation.

In Acts 14:17 Paul talks likewise of the works of nature ordinarily just like a witness of God. We discover this thought in the Old Testament in Psalm 19 and other places.

The following stage in the disclosure of God as identified with sin is his revelation in reason and conscience, or man's discerning (rational) and moral nature. Paul says that the Gentiles, who have not the law, "are a law unto themselves; in that they show work of the law written in their hearts, their conscience bearing witness therewith, and their thoughts one with another accusing or else excusing them" (Rom. 2:14,15). The heart here is presumably a general term signifying about what we mean by moral nature.

It appears that Paul is putting forward that the requirements of the law, in any event for the most part, are uncovered in man's moral consciousness, and that obedience to these prerequisites of the law as in this way made know is for all intents and purposes obedience to the law.

The knowledge of the distinction between right and wrong, with the consciousness that we will bound to do the right and maintain a strategic distance from the wrong, with some knowledge regarding what is right and wrong - this is somewhere around a practical revelation of the moral prerequisites of the law and therefore of the moral nature of God.

To live up to the light accordingly given is so far to keep the law. Not to give up the light in this manner offered is to violate the law and therefore to sin.

A third stage in God's disclosure (revelation) might be meant by the term law. This is Paul's great term when thinking about God's disclosure of himself in relation to man as sinful. By this he implies basically the Old Testament or Mosaic law.

At times he utilizes the term without the article, some of the time with it. With the article obviously he implies the Mosaic law. What's more, without the article he additionally implies fundamentally the Mosaic law, however he is thinking likewise about that law as embodying universal principles of righteousness or moral requirement.

Dr. John Thomas Wylie

When he utilizes the article he is thinking about the Mosaic law more as a solid or concrete system of specific requirements. Without the article the Mosaic law is still as a main priority (it is still in mind) but rather as made up of all universal principles of general application.

The law is the embodiment of the moral requirements of God in published ordinances. The focal point of the Old Testament law looked at as moral prerequisite is the Ten Commandments. The prerequisite of the law is perfect obedience to its mandates. The law thusly allows of no exceptions and makes no provisions for any remissions of penalty.

It condemns without mercy each violator of its precepts. We mean by this the law as moral requirement, which is by all accounts the chief, if not the exclusive, perspective of Paul while discussing about the law in relation to sin.

There was, it is true, provision for ceremonial purging and forgiveness in the Mosaic law. Yet, Paul does not appear to incorporate this aspect of the law in his use of the term; in any event customarily he doesn't, if at any point.

Sin as against the command or moral requirement of the law Paul calls a trespass or transgression. (See Romans 5:12 ff., and other places).

The function of the law in relation to sin was not to justify or to save from sin, but rather to stir one to one's helplessness of sin, to one's weakness in sin, to one's need of the Redeemer, and in this way to serve as the pedagogue to lead the sinner to Christ. (Romans 7; Galatians 3).

The climax of revelation in relation to sin came in the disclosure of the grace of God in Christ which saves from sin. The point we are keen on here isn't the light which we get in this revelation concerning grace, but the light which grace tosses upon sin.

We may get the impression from a few articulations by Paul that the full doctrine of sin came regarding the revelation of the law as a means for developing the nature of sin and giving a knowledge of sin.

Be that as it may, we don't get the complete doctrine of sin until we see the grace of God that saves from sin. The dreadful, awful darkness of sin does not establish its full impression on us until the we see it in contrast to the radiant grace of God and as and as rejection of that grace.

This might be shown on account of Paul himself, who appears to have had a developing consciousness of sin until in his maturity (old age) he considers himself the chief of sinners (I Tim. 1:15). His very own conduct in mistreating (persecuting) the church he thought to be right until he was given the revelation of God's grace. At that point he turned into guilty sinner in his own eyes.

This thought is also illustrated in the teaching of Jesus Christ. Jesus says that because of his presence and teaching in their midst, the cities of his day will receive a greater condemnation than Sodom and Gomorrah (Matt. 11:20 ff.). The servant who has the knowledge of his master's and does it not will be beaten with many stripes, while the servant who knew not his master's will will be beaten with few stripes (Luke 12:47,48).

Once more, Jesus says that if he had not come, the those who reject him had not had sin. Now they have no excuse for their sin (John 15:22). Men are condemned in light of the fact that they love darkness as opposed to light, on the grounds that their deeds are evil (John 3:19). The light of God's grace does two things for the wicked heart;

it uncovers its darkness rather than light, on the grounds that their deeds are evil (John 3:19).

The light of God's grace completes two things for the sinful heart; it uncovers its darkness and it increases that darkness in the event of the individuals who reject the light of grace.

The Johannine compositions (writings) draw out this difference among sin and grace plainly and clearly. Sin is put forward as darkness and hatred and error, while grace is light and love and truth. Between the two there has been a persistent clash (a never ending conflict), and there will keep on being until the point that grace at last conquers sin.

The conflict of things to come (future things to come) is graphically put forward in the book of Revelation, which contains the most distinctive, vivid depiction of the powers of evil in struggle, and conflict with the powers of righteousness to be found anyplace in this writing.

In John's Gospel and First Epistle we discover the differentiation between the darkness of sin and the light of righteousness strikingly presented. What's more, sin takes its last form in unbelief or rejection of Jesus Christ as the Son of God and Savior of the world.

He that believeth not is condemned already, because he hath not believed on the name of the only begotten Son of God (John 3:18). He that disobeyeth the Son shall not see life, but the wrath of God abideth on him (John 3:36). When the Holy Spirit is come, he will convict the world in respect of sin, of righteousness and of judgment (John 16:8 ff.).

Special emphasis in placed upon this last passage for it is worthy of it and we will put a pen here for a moment.

The Holy Spirit's work in convicting concerning righteousness nature is personally identified with his work in convicting concerning sin. Actually, these are not two works but rather just two phases of one convicting work.

This substantiates our position that the final revelation as to sin does not come until the point when we get to the grace of God in Christ. The revelation of righteousness in Jesus Christ uncovers or reveals the nature of sin. The conviction both as to righteousness and to sin centers in Jesus Christ.

The conviction as to judgment consists in the way that the prince of this world has been judged. The devil's judgment of Jesus turns into his very own judgment. The world's judgment of Jesus turned into the world's judgment.

The final judgment of the devilish, diabolical character of sin came in the rejection by the world of the righteous, sinless Son of God. In hence exposing it of all of its embellishments and attractions and showing it up in its actual character, sin was condemned in the eyes of every enlightened moral intelligence.

This again demonstrates the final revelation of the character of sin came in connection with the revelation of the grace of God. Sin crucified the Son of God. But, in doing so, sin always fixed itself (undid itself) in that it forever revealed its very own character as sin.

The conviction as to sin lies in the fact that men believe not on Christ. This most likely means, not that unbelief in Jesus Christ is proof of the world's sin, but that the world's sin consists in its unbelief in him. This position is justified by this passage, as well as by the statements somewhere else in the Johannine compositions (writings) as to unbelief.

It is wherever related to moral darkness. In the First Epistle the liar is the man who denies that Jesus is the Christ (I John 2:22). Maybe the sin is unto death is the final and obdurate rejection of Jesus Christ as the Son of God (I John 5:13-17).

Sin As Unbelief

3. WHAT HAS RECENTLY been said would support the view that unbelief is the essence of sin. This does not mean, in any case, unbelief in the sense of a refusal to accept a doctrine or dogma. It is unbelief in one's rejection of moral and spiritual light, especially as that light is embodied in Jesus Christ.

It is simply the rejection of God's final revelation, his disclosure of himself as made in Jesus Christ. When this rejection winds up unmistakable and willful, it becomes the sin unto death. It is then a willful treading under the foot of the Son of God, counting the blood of the covenant wherewith he sanctified an unholy thing, and doing despite to the Spirit of grace (Heb. 10:29).

It in this manner becomes moral suicide. It is putting out one's own spiritual eyes. It doesn't take place from except in connection with a high degree of enlightenment. It is purposeful or deliberate, willful, malicious rejection of Jesus Christ as God's revelation, knowing that he is such a revelation.

At first sight this does not appear to concur with what Jesus says about blasphemy against the Holy Spirit, since he says that all sins and blasphemies shall be forgiven, however not the blasphemy against the Holy Spirit (Matt. 12:22 ff.).

If we remember that the sin that men were committing which led Jesus to utter this warning was the sin of attributing his works to the power of the devil, thus denying that they were wrought by the power of God, at that point he isn't thinking of sin or blasphemy against the Spirit irrespective of the Spirit's relation to the Father or the Son.

He is thinking about the Spirit as epitomized or embodied in his very own life and works and along these lines uncovering the presence of God, giving men light to see and recognize God in him. When men along these lines enlightened by the Spirit purposely reject his works as the works of God and attribute them to the devil, they blaspheme the Spirit, and there is never forgiveness for their sin.

This is basically unbelief in its final form as put forward by John and willful sin as described in Hebrews.

Some have defined the basic rule of sin as selfishness-not selfishness as opposed to kindheartedness, benevolence toward one's fellow man, however selfishness in the sense of the assertion of one's own will as opposed to the submission to the will of God.

To live in sin, at that point, is to carry on with a real existence focused in "self," to erect one's own will as the law of life. This, it is said, is appeared to be the essential principle of sin in the fact that love to God is the essence of virtue. Hence, the opposite must be the essence of sin.

Once more, the way that Jesus made the first condition of discipleship to be self-denial refusal would show that selfishness is the basic guideline of sin. But, selfishness as along these lines characterized is for all intents and purposes is practically the same thing from unbelief as set forth above.

Each is simply the principle of self-assertion as opposed to humble submission and trust in God. Each is defiance, and rebellious against God. Each is essentially a similar thing that John had as a primary concern when he said that sin is lawlessness. Furthermore, infringement or violation of the moral order set up by God is rebellion against God.

Sin Is Against God As A Person

4. THINK ABOUT ANOTHER phase of the doctrine of sin. In some cases sin is mulled over as an infringement or violation of the moral order or law, sometimes it is considered as a personal offense against God. At any rate, Paul sees it in relation to the law.

He imagines nature, man's heart and conscience, and the entire Old Testament revelation as an expression of the righteous will of God in an objective moral order.

Sin is an infringement or violation of this moral order and brings upon man the anger of God. It isn't necessary that there ought to be a composed law whose commands man shall abuse or violate so as to bring upon himself the fury, the wrath of a righteous God. He may sin against God who reveals himself in nature and man's own moral constitution. When he does so, he expedites himself the condemnation of a holy God.

In other places sin is thought of as a personal offense against God. This turns out in Psalm 51:4 when the essayist, taking a look at the hugeness of his sin, says: "Against thee, thee only, have I sinned, and done that which is evil in thy sight."

Dr. John Thomas Wylie

The writer does not imply that he has not sinned against his fellow man, but rather intends to assert in emphatic form that his sin is first of all against God.

What has quite recently been said, in any case, demonstrates that sin in its final and most lethal form is sin against a personal God revealed in Jesus Christ as a God of mercy and love.

Sin As Guilt

5. VIEWING SIN AS personal ill desert, we portray it by the expression "guilt."

There is likely no single term in the Old or New Testament indicating only this thought, but the idea goes entirely through the two divisions of the Bible. The feeling of disgrace, shame and ill desert caused Adam to dress himself with fig leaves and conceal himself from his Maker (Gen. 3:8).

Adam attempted to move the fault (blame, guilt) to his better half, and Eve thus to the snake; but for each situation there was obviously the feeling of ill desert.

The guilt of sin shows itself in consciousness. Man knows himself as blameworthy by virtue of his sin. This consciousness of ill desert is a general marvel of human life, particularly of man's religious life. This is true despite the fact that there is a general demeanor to shroud one's sense of ill desert and conceal or reject one's responsibility for sin.

Truth be told, the endeavor to conceal one's guilt is itself proof of guilt. A clear consciousness is not so quick to endeavor to legitimize itself as a guilty one. This sense of guilt shows itself likewise in the fact that men point the finger at each other with reference to their deeds.

The longing to legitimize oneself in one's own eyes and according to others prompts much "rationalization," or giving of false purposes (reasons) behind one's beliefs and conduct. One may regularly believe that the false reasons, given to oneself and to other people, are the genuine reasons when they are definitely not. One may deceive himself just as others by such rationalization.

This consciousness of ill desert, then, isn't to be taken as the precise proportion of the guilt of sin. This is true with reference to one's very own sin or to another's. Our moral decisions (judgments) are not any more reliable than are our judgments in other realms.

Indeed, usually the case that the reverse is true, in particular, that the more noteworthy (greater) one's guilt, the less he is aware (conscious) of it. This is true in view of the blinding power of sin. Sin darkens the spiritual vision and twists the moral judgment.

Subsequently, presumably the most unsafe condition that one can be in spiritually is to have no consciousness of sin and no sense of peril. For one to have no feeling of ill desert is not a sign that one is without guilt; it is an indication that he is spiritually blind and in great spiritual danger.

The closer one gets to God, the more conscious he is of his own unworthiness. Then again, if that we state that we have no sin, we deceive ourselves and the truth is not in us (I John 1:8). Self-conscious goodness is constantly sham goodness. It is spoiled at the center (rotten to the core).

This was one of the exceptional characteristics of the Pharisees. They expressed gratitude toward God that they were not like other men. They turned up their noses at "publicans and sinners."

They scorned, and despised Jesus for associating with such human driftwood.

But, these self-righteous Pharisees were the men that Jesus condemned most bitterly. He scorched them with the fires of his righteous indignation. Then again is Paul who in his maturity (old age) considered himself the chief of sinners (I Tim. 1:15), and counted not that he had attained perfection (Phil. 3:12,13).

The ground of guilt, nonetheless, is the relation of man as ill deserving to the holiness of God. Man's sin is ill deserving in light of the fact that it is against God as holy. If God were not holy, sin would not be ill deserving. The origination of any religion with regards to the character of transgression (sin) is determined principally by its conception of the character of God.

It is against the foundation of God's unblemished character that the blackness of sin is to be seen. This is the reason the righteous man see his very own sin so clearly, in light of the fact that he sees his sin over against the character of God. The prophet sees Jehovah high and lifted up, the exalted and Holy One.

At that point he sees himself and the people among whom he lives as corrupt, sinful.

The perfection of God's character is presumably the fundamental conception of the First Epistle of John. God is light and love. In contrast to the perfection of his character the essayist sees with distinctness man's sin. If any man says that he has no transgression (sin), he hoodwinks himself (deceives himself) and the truth is not in him.

Men are not equally guilty before God. In the Old Testament there were sins of ignorance and sins of presumption; sins that could be atoned for by penances (sacrifices) and sins that put one outside the covenant relation to God.

Jesus perceives this principle. The people of Sodom and Gomorrah won't have as overwhelming condemnation as the urban communities which had the advantage of his ministry and teaching (Matt. 11:20 ff.).

The servant who know not his master's shall not have the same punishment as the person who knows but does not (Luke 12:47,48). Paul perceives the same principle. Men are held responsible for the light they have, regardless of whether that light be the light of nature, of the heart and conscience, or of the Old Testament law (Romans 1-2).

It seems, that light and privilege are components that go into the determination of the level of one's guilt. The level of one's guilt may be said to be determined by the proportion of wilfulness that goes into one's sinning (Heb. 10:26 ff.). To the extent that one sins wilfully, to that extent is one guilty and his character settled (fixed) in sin.

It is now and then said that ignorance is no excuse, and the implication is that the ignorant are as guilty as the individuals who have more prominent light and privilege. Be that as it may, this won't hold. The instance of Paul is now and then referred to demonstrate that one may act ignorantly but then be guilty.

Paul seems to infer here that he was honest but then liable. Be that as it may, Paul likewise says that since he did what he did ignorantly in unbelief, God showed mercy toward him. This obviously suggests his ignorance changed his guilt (I Tim. 1:13).

This principle is recognized in the social relations of life. The man with light, benefit, opportunity, ability, is held to a stricter record by his kindred men. Official courtrooms consider the component of deliberateness in a man's crime in evaluating his punishment.

Sin As Depravity

6. ANOTHER PHASE OF transgression (sin) is portrayed by the expression "depravity."

A. By this term is implied that state or condition of man's moral nature that makes it not just conceivable that he may sin because of his power of choice, but sure that he will sin by virtue of his moral shortcoming (weakness) and inalienable tendency toward evil.

This depravity of man's nature is inherent and all universal. These two thoughts - the possibility that debasement is natural and that it is all inclusive - appear to be indistinguishable (inseparable).

Absolutely, if sin is inherent, it is universal; and, then again, in the event that it is universal, there is a solid presumption that it is inherent. By saying that sin is a constituent component in human nature, or that sin and human nature are indistinguishable (inseparable).

Human nature was not created corrupt, sinful or depraved. Jesus Christ did not have a depraved human nature. In addition, if sin were a constituent component in human nature, man couldn't be saved from sin.

In any case, in saying that depravity is characteristic in human nature is implied that man as fallen is brought into the world depraved; that since Adam's time and because of the Fall all men are brought into the world with such an moral tendency toward sin that it is a moral certainty, that it is morally inescapable, that when they come to settle on moral choices, they will commit sin.

b. That "depravity" is inborn is confirmed by the accompanying realities:

a. The immediate teaching of the Scriptures. In Psalm 51 the author says: "In sin did my mother conceive me" (Psalm 51:5). Jeremiah says: "The heart is deceitful and desperately devilish; who can know it?" (Jer. 17:9).

Paul says that we are naturally the children of wrath (Eph. 2:3). Some claim that Paul isn't here alluding to the inborn disposition because of the fact that in the setting he is examining the course of life as sinful.

Consequently it is said that he isn't discussing an inborn depravity, however a course of actual

Dr. John Thomas Wylie

transgression. Actually, he is discussing a course of life, however it is a course of life as growing out of and as communicating the inborn depravity.

It is a native disposition developing in its natural course into a natural course into a life of sin. The life of sin is disclosed by alluding it to the native moral disposition. Men are commonly the offspring of wrath as in their lives of transgression, which incur the wrath of God, are the natural outgrowth of their native disposition.

b. Another reality that demonstrates that depravity is inherent in the sense shown above, is the way that it is universal. That transgression (sin) is universal is clearly taught in the Bible.

In Genesis, following the sin of the first man, there is the concentrated and broad development of sin until the point that the race before long became so corrupt that God sent a flood and decimated the race aside from Noah and his family.

While Noah was a man of faith, he was an exceptionally defective man or a imperfect man. It is clarified that no man in scriptural history was sinless, aside from Jesus himself. They absolute best men of both Old and New Testament times were feeble and sinful.

The psalmist represents God as searching the earth, but discovering none without transgression (Psalm 14: 1 ff.). Jesus viewed all men as sinful. He says: "If ye, being evil" (Luke 11:13). This articulation demonstrates that he regards all men as evil and sinful. He teaches, as one of the principal things in prayer, that men ought to appeal to God for forgiveness (Matt. 6:12).

They require forgiveness as universally as they require every day bread. Paul unequivocally encourages that all men are sinners. All have sinned (Rom. 3:9 ff.). This presupposition underlies his argument in Romans 5:12 ff.

Experience, observation, and mankind's history demonstrate that sin is universal. The best of men admit themselves delinquents (sinners). Nor is this to be translated as the aftereffect of an abnormal or grim awareness on their part.

Men who, similar to Paul, Luther, and John Bunyan, remain at the focal point of spiritual Christianity, can't be viewed as entirely misconstruing their own relation to God.

The accord among men is that no man lives above moral and spiritual blame. The course of mankind's history demonstrates that there is something in a general sense amiss with humanity.

The best clarification of the universality of sin is to clarify it by alluding it to the corruption of human nature in the beginning of mankind's history. The Bible offers us to comprehend that the first man abused God's communicated will and by doing as such the flood of mankind's history was corrupted at its source.

c. The question has been discussed with respect as to whether man is totally depraved. That depends inside and out on the meaning of total depravity. If by total depravity is implied that man is as degenerate or corrupt as he can be, then positively the doctrine isn't true.

But in the sense that in man is absolutely defenseless, (helpless) as a result of his natural inheritance, outside the provisions of God's saving grace, the doctrine is true. The issue may be summed up by saying that man is totally depraved in the accompanying sense:

a. As in man's whole nature, every component and faculty of his being, has been weakened and corrupted by sin. Life elements (body, soul, spirit) have gone under its power. Man's mind has been darkened, his heart depraved, his will perverted by sin.

b. It implies that man is absolutely unable to deliver himself from the power of sin. Here is the crux of the issue. The truth for which the term total depravity stands is simply the total inability of man to save himself, his whole helplessness is in the grip of sin.

c. Without divine help man turns out to become worse and more worse. Rather than total depravity implying that man is as awful as he can be, it implies that, without the redeeming power of God's grace, he will everlastingly sink deeper and deeper, further and further into sin.

A significant part of the disagreement about the total depravity has been aside the mark, because it depended on the predisposition that what made sin deadly was the extent to which man was influenced by it.

Sin was viewed as ruinous provided the sin was sufficiently huge enough. But it isn't the extent of sin that makes it dangerous or deadly;

it is the nature of sin. Sin slaughters since it is sin, sin kills because it is sin, not on the grounds that it is enormous. The very nature of sin is such that it would dethrone God and introduce moral and spiritual anarchy into God's universe.

Consequently, no sin can be tolerated in man. The very nature of sin is such that the end goal that it poisons man's moral nature and ruin his spiritual life. It cuts man off from God.

Sin As Bondage

WE HAVE NOTICED THAT transgression creates a state of moral shortcoming (weakness) from which man is absolutely unable to deliver himself.

Jesus and Paul underscore the bondage of sin. Jesus says that the man who submits sin is the slave (captive) of sin (John 8:34). In one place he says that the truth will free from this bondage; in another, the Son (John 8:32, 36).

Paul puts forth in Romans 6 that man is either the servant of sin or of God and righteousness. In chapter seven he gives his a vivid account of his very own struggle with the power of sin, of his express powerlessness or inability to deliver himself, and of his finding deliverance in Jesus Christ.

There appear to be three unmistakable stages as far as Paul can tell as put forth in this chapter. The first is a state which he discusses as being alive without the law (v. 9a). He had no cognizance of judgment and death, since he had not been stirred by the law to a knowledge of its demands.

The second stage is one in which he ends up mindful of the righteous demands of the law, but can't satisfy its demands. "The commandment came, sin revived, and I died" (v. 9b). This prompts a sense of absolute powerlessness, utter helplessness and after that to lose hope (to despair).

At long last comes the realization of deliverance through Jesus Christ (v. 25). This reigning principle of sin Paul perceives as being universal, as shown in chapter five.

It is a pathetic depiction that Paul gives us in Romans 7 of a man divided against himself. He perceives the good, he has desires after the good, but he can't attain it.

He is pulled apart. Such a man can never accomplish the good. Also, his personality can't be so bound together in reaching after the good until it is brought together around a person, Jesus

Christ. Until the point when Christ comes in and takes possession, sin rules. A greater power must drive out sin, and Jesus Christ alone is that greater power.

Such a case as Paul depicts in this chapter is pitiable, yet not the most regrettable using any and all means. He portrays the man with an exclusive requirement of good and bad (the law), with a delicate still, small voice and a sharp desire to do the right and win God's support.

Be that as it may, he doesn't have the ability to accomplish what he tries to be and do. He falls flat and ends up aware of his disappointment. There are other men who have no such sharp feeling of good and bad, no high moral and religious guidelines, and no earnest desire to do the good as they do see it.

They are the ones who, if they perceive the good, do as such just in sort of moronic form. Maybe every person perceives the good to some degree, but some appear to do as such just faintly. Furthermore, this acknowledgment turns out to be increasingly obscured.

Obviously, we need to perceive that multiple occasions there are stirrings in the human heart of which we see no outward sign. In any case, there likewise seem to be numerous individuals who give themselves over increasingly more unreasonably to sin.

They turn out to be progressively the captives of sin. Evil an ever increasing number of rules the inner life just as the external. Truth be told, as Jesus shows us, it is the dominance of wickedness, evil over the inward life that is the most wretched piece of the picture.

The tree is awful, and henceforth the fruit is terrible. A few men are claimed by evil until, as Paul says, they come to "work all uncleanness with greediness" (Eph. 4:19).

Sin As An Evil Heart

IN THIS MANNER JESUS stresses sin similar to an internal matter of thought and motive. When the Pharisees reprimanded his disciples for eating with unwashed hands, Jesus revealed to them that it was not that which goes into a man that contaminates him, however that which originates from inside, from the heart (moral nature) of the man.

Dr. John Thomas Wylie

He at that point specifies evil contemplations and a wide range of insidiousness (Mark 7:1 ff.). He makes sin to be both internal and external. It involves the whole man, the external deed, yet the deed as uncovering and communicating the internal life. The man is then overall increasingly more overwhelmed by evil. Man in making a decision about his individual man is to a great extent restricted to the outward demonstration; God makes a decision about the heart.

Here as wherever human life must be judged from within to be judged truly. To look only on the outward act is to miss the significance of the issue. Sin is a deed; but it is in excess of a act seen from without; it is a personal deed, and a person acts from within.

Sin is a deed committed by a person, and a person acts from within provoked by a moral motive. The moral quality of the deed lies in the nature of the intention or motive. So Jesus deciphers murder and infidelity (Matt. 5:21 ff., 27 ff.).

The moral quality of the deed has a place preferably with the person rather than to the deed as a act considered basically as a act. The moral quality of the man decides the quality of the deed as opposed to that the deed decides the nature of the man. Obviously, the deed indicates the man, but the man decides the deed. The tree decides the organic product, fruit; and the fruit marks the tree as good or bad.

So the inner and outward life of the man constitute a unity. One can't be isolated from the other. Obviously, a terrible man may reenact the ethics of the great man; however, all things being equal, his reproduction is the outflow of a double-dealing and devilish heart.

To make the fruit good, the tree should initially be made good. A man, at that point, might be a killer on the most fundamental level without really killing anyone. He that hates his brother is a murderer (I John 3:15). John is discussing hatred as a settled and governing guideline in one's life.

If hatred turns into the governing guideline of one's life with the goal that he would murder his brother in the event that open door emerged, he is a killer, a murderer whether he commits the deed or not.

The equivalent applies to infidelity or adultery, to stealing, to lying, and to every other type of sin.

Dr. John Thomas Wylie

The evil of the man makes the deed evil. Sin is in excess of act; it is a condition of character. Committing the deed will affirm and fix the character in evil; however it is the evil heart (whole, inner moral of life of man) that makes the deed evil, wicked.

Chapter

TWO

Original Sin

A Preliminary Survey

1. THE SUBJECT OF original sin has been tremendously talked about. The certainties to be represented are when all is said in done two: man's inborn moral depravity, and, also, the comprehensiveness of transgression. These are the realities of essential moment to man. These actualities don't rely on a specific clarification with respect to how they became.

They are not two certainties, but rather two parts of one dim and dreadful reality - the reign of sin in human life and history. Paul in Romans 5 associates the all inclusive rule of sin and death with the transgression of Adam.

Numerous hypotheses have been designed about how we are identified with Adam's sin in such a route as, to the point that his transgression became the means or ground of our condemnation and death. Paul himself offers no theory of the issue. He just affirms the fact.

The most basic and characteristic clarification is that, since Adam was the natural head and wellspring of the race, the race in general acquires a depraved nature from him. As such, the reality of sin and death as a widespread marvel in human life is followed back to Adam's sin as the reason or source.

The relation among Adam and his relatives is essentially that of leader of the race and individuals who spring from him. With regards to the imputation of Adam's sin as an act of sin to the individual members from the race, no hypothesis or theory of such ascription is required, for the basic reason that there was no such imputation.

The possibility that Adam's sin as an act of sin is charged to his relatives and on that account they are liable and thus denounced, is an idea too ridiculous to even consider being truly engaged.

The Augustinian And Federal Theories

2. THE AUGUSTINIAN THEORY is that since men were fundamentally present in Adam, or present with regards to the substance of their being, they, in this manner, partook in his transgression, and on that ground the sin was charged to them. They are, in this manner, blameworthy of Adam's transgression (sin), since they partook in it.

Since the transgression is credited to them and they are blameworthy of it, they are brought into the world debased and censured. Without a doubt of it, this theory respects in extremely rough and materialistic way the possibility of Adam's relatives being available in him.

There is no sense in which Adam's relatives can be viewed as having been available in him in order to legitimize the ascription of Adam's sin to them.

The Federal Theory is no better. It says that God made a covenant with Adam, the terms of which were that on state of Adam's obedience to God his relatives ought to have everlasting life; on state of his rebellion his sin ought to be charged to them, and thus they would be blameworthy and denounced.

There isn't a sliver of proof from the Bible that any such covenant was ever constructed with Adam. Someone has well said that the agreement started in Holland as opposed to in the Garden of Eden. Such a charging of the transgressions of one human individual to another on the ground of a covenant, with which the one to whom sin is charged had nothing to do, would be the stature of shamefulness, injustice.

Race Unity

3. THERE IS, BE that as it may, an organic unity of the race which definitely results in the members suffering with and for each other. God created the race as a race, not as disconnected and separated units. Original sin implies that the race as a race, and all its individual members have fallen.

Each man is naturally introduced to a fallen race and shares its fallen state. If one objects to this on the ground that one member should not suffer over another's bad behavior, or wrongdoing the appropriate response is this is a law of life, regardless of what we may say about it.

It's anything but a question with respect to whether we figure it ought to have been that way or not. Actually, it is that way. What's more, it must be that way if there is to be any social life for man. A plan as indicated by which each man emerged as a separated, isolated unit. There would be no social life in the course of such an arrangement. Nor could there be any such thing as one man appreciating, or enjoying the advantages of another's work or goodness.

Not exclusively would there be no social evil; there could be no social good. Each man would suffer with unyielding, numerical exactness the exact desert of this possess his own deeds and no one could help him.

The best social thought of our times emphasizes this aspect of both sin and righteousness; in particular, that others are influenced or affected by either. No man can draw himself off into a corner and live to himself so that no one else is worried with regards to the sort of life that he lives.

Others are concerned, crucially concerned. While sin, as before expressed, is fundamentally against God, this truth has once in a while been translated in such an uneven path as to establish the impression that only God and the individual soul are concerned in one's sin.

But sin is a social affair. There is no such thing as a person in the sense of a segregated and inconsequential unit. No sin n its consequences is ever restricted to the soul that commits it. Sin is against God. But God has established a social and moral order. This order in which men live respectively is abused, violated by man's sin.

The doctrine of original sin implies that man isn't only a social being, however that the race is an organic unity, and as an organic unity it was influenced by the sin of the first man, the head of the race. Through the law of natural generation, the whole race has inherited the evil effects of that first transgression. All men have been conceived on a lower moral and spiritual plane than they would have been if Adam had not sinned.

This insidious entail of transgression (sin) has been passed down by social influence as well as by natural inheritance. Sin is self-proliferating (self-influence). It has ruined (corrupted) the whole social environment of the race and has entered each phase of the life of man.

No part of man's life is untouched by it. Every human relation and every single social foundation have been infested by the power of sin and the defilement, corruption delivered by it. If anyone challenges that depravity can involve natural inheritance one thing is sure; to be specific, that the corrupting power of moral evil is found all through the whole extent of man's life. This is true regardless of specific means with respect to how it happened.

Dr. John Thomas Wylie

Individual Responsibility In Relation To Race Unity

1. A LARGE PORTION of the trouble in this inquiry has become out of the push to fathom the theoretical question with respect to whether the individual was liable by virtue of that first sin and to what degree and on what ground.

So far as individual responsibility and blame (guilt) for an act committed thousands of years before one was conceived and with which he didn't have anything to do. I am all the more exclusively dependable, and consequently blameworthy, for what Adam did than I am for what Augustus Caesar did. Be that as it may, I am affected in my life by what both did.

Organic, social, and historical impacts have bound my life up with what they did. With regards to the justice of an order of things in which that should be true, I will be unable to work that out.

There are theoretical difficulties. It might be hard to see how I should be responsible for deeds which grow out of and express a nature which I inherited. In the event that I am not responsible for the nature, how might I be responsible for the deeds which unavoidably grow out of it?

2. In reply to this trouble a few things might be stated:

a. The first is that whatever theory one may hold as to Adam's transgression and our relation to it, the fact appears to stand that, when we come to the age of moral consciousness and moral activity, we wind up so related to evil driving forces within us and evil social powers around us that we are as of now slaves to them, or down to earth captives to them.

These insidious powers did not originate in acts of our own will. This may appear to be a fact of dark and foreboding perspective, but we can't dispose of it by denying its existence. Unpleasant actualities are not discarded by denying their right to be or by calling them by metaphorical names. Men have attempted sufficiently long enough to heal the world's moral corruption by this sort of word jugglery.

b. The second actuality to be observed is that both the Scriptures and moral consciousness

Dr. John Thomas Wylie

bear testimony to our obligation regarding our lives in spite of our inherited natures. Truth be told, this evil inheritance is viewed in the Bible as constituting a part of our dreadful condition, calling for divine grace and help.

The testimony of our moral consciousness on this point can't be doubted. As evil and sinful self, we recognize our unfortunate state and renounce the sinful self. One must deny this sinful self, take up one's cross, be crucified with Jesus Christ, in order to live.

c. In the third place, there is general agreement among all classes of zealous scholars, legitimized by standards drawn from the New Testament and from our christian cognizance, that all inability up to the point of positive transgression and intentional rejection of good light is provided for in the redeeming work of Jesus Christ.

There is race redemption as well as race sin. No man, in this manner, will be lost just on account of original or race sin. Up to the point of positive transgression or rejection of moral light, the individual is provided for in the grace of God without personal repentance and faith.

Somebody might be unsatisfied now on the ground that it leaves a borderland in which we can't advise with regards to the condition and predetermination of the person. That is true. It leaves a borderland. In any case, it makes sensibly clear the principles whereupon which God deals with men.

As to deciding the fate of the individual, we need not give ourselves any undue concern about that, since it isn't our business. It is made plain in the New Testament that the man who rejects clear gospel light is lost.

The man who unquestionably accepts the grace of God is saved. As to the individuals who fall in between, we can securely leave them in the hands of God. Since that is the place their fate at long last rests, that is the thing that we will probably do, regardless of whether we will or not. The only relation we have to the issue is to carry the light of the gospel to all men, with the goal that their responsibility in the matter will be as definite as possible.

With respect to choosing matters which rest in the hands of God, he can most likely do that superior to anything we can. The best manner for us to clear ourselves in the matter is to do what he has plainly revealed as his will.

As to deciding who is lost and who isn't, regardless of whether we can't choose on account of each person, it is clear with regards to the difference in standing before God of the individuals who reject clear gospel light and the individuals who accept it.

As has been well stated, despite the fact that we can't push in a blade cutting edge at the exact point that isolates day and night and state that here one finishes and alternate starts, still the difference between light and darkness is genuinely clear.

Conclusion As To The Moral Condition And Salvation Of The Infant

5. WITH REGARDS TO the subject of newborn child salvation (or infant salvation), it is commonly concurred among zealous scholars that those withering in early stages are saved. This isn't held such a great amount on the ground that there is explicit Scripture teaching with that effect as it is a result of certain general standards in gospel

teaching as to God's dealings with men, and as a result of the general perspective of the character of God as revealed in Jesus Christ.

There are a few positions on this question of the condition and fate of the child that might be summed up in a nutshell proclamations.

One position might be placed in the explanation that the child is an angel. In any case, the child isn't an angel, utilizing that term to symbolize a guiltless, unfallen being. The child is corrupted in nature and conceivably a transgressor of God's law.

Another position might be summed up in the explanation that the child is a devil. In any case, that isn't true. The possibility of a demon or devil is a being wholly determined toward evil, thus without driving forces to good that even the grace of God couldn't change its character.

Another explanation that outlines the situation of many is that the child is an animal.

The youngster is an animal, yet substantially more. In the event that the child were just an animal, it could never wind up fit for good life and character.

The child has the limit of forming into a moral peresonality. It doesn't have the forces and limits of personality at first, however typically these develop. In that sense the child transcends above the creature. It doesn't have the created forces of personality, however its typical destiny is to develop into personality. In that sense it is personal.

Additionally, there are such needs of evil tendency in the child's nature, and such social influences for evil in the world in which the child experience that it unavoidably commits transgressions when it comes to the age of moral responsibility.

It that sense the child is a sinner. It doesn't have personal guilt. That is inconceivable where the conditions of moral responsibility are inadequate. These are missing in the child's life until the powers of self-consciousness and self-determination arise. There can be no personal guilt except in the case of a personal agent.

In view of these considerations we believe that we are justified in holding that the child dying in infancy is saved. In other words, where there has been cognizant and positive recognizable proof of oneself with evil, there must be likewise, under the grace of God, cognizant and positive denial of evil and ID of oneself with right before there can be redemption from evil. Up to the point of positive distinguishing proof of oneself with right or wrong, there is only the potentiality of moral life.

On account of the child, that possibly is evil aside from the positive influence of the grace of God in redeeming from this evil potentiality or the life of transgression that becomes out of it.

So far as the bowed of the child's nature and the social influences of the world order are concerned, these are toward abhorrence. To save the child from this evil inheritance requires the grace of God, which transcends nature and the world order.

In the event that anybody should raise the complaint that this makes gospel light a risky or dangerous thing, in that it might be the means for heavier judgment, we allow the protest, as well as urge that it is valid. Be that as it may, all ethical light is perilous.

The most benevolent powers in the world, when appropriately utilized, turn into the most hazardous when we are badly acclimated to them. The nurturing powers of air, water, and light progressed toward becoming life-obliterating unless wisely controlled and directed. wrongly coordinated moves toward becoming obscurity and demise.

Dr. John Thomas Wylie

Intelligence wrongly directed becomes darkness and death. The grace of God, when rejected, becomes unceasing passing and hopeless destruction. To be a person with moral opportunities and obligations is itself an unsafe thing. However, who might, along these lines, care to sink to the dimension of the savage?

Thusly, the powers that make for the development of personality are risky powers. The most elevated of these is the grace of God that saves from sin. Be that as it may, so far as should be obvious, even God can't make and create personality without running the risk involved. He can't present his grace to man with a view to his salvation without running the risk of having men reject that grace and in this manner incur condemnation.

The Results of Sin

4. PORTIONS OF THE things treated here as consequences of sin should maybe have been considered as being of the nature of sin. Be that as it may, regardless of whether they be considered

as results or of the precise pith of sin, they are inseparable from it.

In the moral order of the world, sin and the things here talked about have a place together. Some of them are all the more unmistakably of the nature of results, however others may be viewed as more about as of sin's very embodiment or essence.

Sin Alienates From God

1. IT IS OF the very nature of transgression (sin) to distance man from God. In the story of the prodigal son (which) may should be known as the illustration of the loving father, Jesus educates us regarding the more youthful child who accumulated all together and withdrew for a far nation. Here we have a clear picture of sin and its ruin. Sin is a leaving from whole being against God and close God out of man's life.

This leaving from God, or estrangement from God, isn't, in any case, an aloof demeanor; it is certain antagonistic vibe toward God. Paul discusses the carnal minded personality of man.

By this he implies man's mind as unrenewed by the Spirit of God.

He says that this carnal mind is hatred against God. It isn't liable to the law of God; it can't be. To be in this manner subject to the law is in opposition to its moral nature (Rom. 8:7).

In the Garden of Eden, after Adam defied God, in his disgrace, in his shame, he concealed himself from God (Gen. 3:8ff.). Man has been acting along these lines from that point forward. Sin closes man out from God's presence and drives God out of man's life.

One of the most instructive passages in the New Testament on sin is Romans 1:18-32.

Paul lets us know there how the invisible God reveals himself to men through the things that are made. Then he shows that men, "knowing God, glorified him not as God, neither gave thanks." He indicates that they "refused to have God in their knowledge."

Be that as it may, they didn't surrender religion. Their religion rather was corrupted, degraded. They progressed toward becoming worshipers of another god (idolaters). They worshiped the images of corruptible man, of feathered creatures, of four-footed beasts and creeping things. They worshiped the creature instead of the eternal Creator of all things.

This may be a sign of what Paul implies when in Ephesians (2:12) he discusses men as "without God in the world" (truly, "atheists in the world"). Maybe he implies that they are without a knowledge of the true God. He is speaking here as in Romans 1:18-32 of the condition of the Gentile world.

They don't have the foggiest idea about the true God. But in vanity of their minds (Rom. 1:21,22) they invent substitutes for him, and false religion replaces true religion. Paul did not think that one religion was good as another. History proves that religion might be a degrading power in human life as well as an elevating power. Sin lays its disgusting hand on the altar of man's worship and befouls it.

Sin Degrades The Sinner

2. PAUL REVEALS TO us that no man lives to himself (Rom. 14:7). This is regularly interpreted as meaning that in what we do we are identified with others and should, in this way, be careful

about such relations. Paul teaches that a man ought to have a mind to his relations to other people and particularly with regards to the influence of his life on others.

He makes that point in this chapter, but that isn't his point that he says that no man lives to himself. He proceeds to state that no man dies to himself. So he says that whether we live or die we are the Lord's.

Man's life and personality are grounded in God. We have recently observed that sin estranges or alienates from God. Since sin cuts the underlying foundations of man's fellowship with God, it makes his personality wither and die.

In prevalent language, when we speak about man's personality or of his personal power, we are thinking about his social activities. We have schools that guarantee in a couple of simple lessons to disclose to one how to build up his personality in order to have the ability to influence other individuals and motivate them to do what he needs done.

In any case, this is somewhat shallow. Once in a while what it adds up to is figuring out how to conceal one's narrow minded goals (selfish intentions) and make oneself lovely enough to have the ability to trick the other individual.

The underlying foundations of one's personal being are in one's fellowship with God, the Creator and Sustainer of all of us. To nourish one's fellowship with God, therefore, is the best means for building up one's personality. Furthermore, whatever breaks that fellowship will make one's personality to shrink and die.

Fellowship with God is as necessary and fundamental for the improvement of personality as air and daylight are for the development of blooms. Also, let us not bamboozle ourselves here. We are not to look for fellowship with God for the goal of developing personality.

There may sneak in here a subtle, unpretentious spiritual selfishness that will be self-defeating. God isn't to be degraded into the position of being used for our selfish ends- - even alleged spiritual ends. We should find our end in God, not seek to make him the means of carrying out our ends.

By information disclosed above, we don't intend to state that the aggravation of social relations brought about by sin isn't degrading to personality. The rupture of such relations because of sin degrades man's personal powers. We were certifying that personality is grounded in God, and to be cut off from God dwarfs personality.

In any case, it is likewise true that personality is begotten in a social matrix, is developed in social relations and must be kept up in social activity. Therefore, sin degrades personality, both in light of the fact that it cuts man off from fellowship with God and upsets his relations with his colleagues.

It is simple enough to perceive how arousing sins (sensual sins) obliterate man's personal powers, but it isn't always so apparent this is true on account of progressively refined and so-called spiritual forms of sin.

However, regardless of whether apparent without a moment's delay or not obvious by any means, all forms of sin are corrupting, degrading to personality. All forms of sin will in general close one up in a packaging of selfishness that shuts out God and one's colleagues.

Self-centered personality dies. It can live only in an atmosphere of fellowship - fellowship with God and with one's kindred men. Turned in on itself it dies.

The first demand of discipleship is the discipline of self-denial. One must revoke self-power. He should give himself over to Another. One can't begin to act normally until he comes to Jesus Christ as Lord.

It is instructive to take a passage (one out of numerous such in the New Testament) like Ephesians 4:17-19 and note a portion of the articulations Paul uses to depict the course of the sinful life.

Notice a portion of these articulations: "the vanity of their mind"; "darkened in their understanding"; "because of the ignorance that is in them"; "because of the hardening of their heart." Here we have articulations that describe precisely the deterioration, debasement, and degradation that come to personality because of a life of sin.

A few people assume that except if some outside catastrophe comes to pass for a man when he sins, he isn't being punished for his sin. In any case, the most horrendous discipline does not come as outer cataclysm, but rather as the internal collapse of his personal powers and capacities.

The most terrible cataclysm or calamity that goes to a man is the thing that occurs in the man himself. Emerson contends, in substance, in one place, that many people circumnavigate the globe to get away from their misery but can't do so such because they cannot get away from themselves. "Myself am hell."

One phase of this corruption, this sin, this degradation of the sinner's personality is the self-deluding power of sin. Whatever form one's transgression may take, it will in turns the sinner over upon himself so he winds up beguiled, even infatuated by his very own ideas, plans, and purposes.

We have seen that temptation always appears in the pretense of a good. Else it would be no temptation. Also, when one yields to temptation and enjoys sin, generally speaking, he doesn't take learn wisdom from the experience and renounce his evil course.

Usually the opposite is true. The sinner winds up blinded and deluded. Some men have contended that involvement in sin would be the solution for sin; that by encountering the severe consequences of sin, men would revoke sin and follow after righteousness.

Some of the time, by the grace of God, this has been true. Be that as it may, it ought to be noticed, that, when this happens, it is because of the grace of God, and not to wisdom that originated from indulging in sin. Indulging in sin does not give wisdom; it only generates folly.

It doesn't open one's eyes to truth; it blinds with the goal that one can't see truth. What men now and again take for wisdom learned from a godless life is just visually impaired blind arrogance that implies folly and ruin. Professing themselves to be wise, they moved toward becoming blockheads, as the Scripture says, "fools."(Rom. 1:22).

In this way sin is foolish, and is self-defeating. This is exemplified in the lives of the those who make their chief purpose in life the quest for material merchandise.

One who strives after material goods as his chief object turns out to be increasingly more engaged in the quest for things and loses the sense of the value of spiritual things.

His heart turns out to be increasingly more set on things. Where one's treasures are, there will his heart be (Matt. 6:21). If one engaged in pursuit of the quest for material riches as his chief end fails in getting riches, he ends up frustrated and hopeless, in light of the fact that he neglects to get what he most desires throughout everyday life.

He fails in his chief point throughout everyday life and dies defeated. Then again, in the event that he prevails with regards to securing riches, he will discover, as Jesus taught that life does not consist in the abundance of the things that one possesses (Luke 12:15).

Such a man had thought, that the ownership of things would give bliss and wealth of life. Now he finds that it does not. What he thought he wanted he may in any case still want. Like the misery gloating and boasting over his gold, he may in any case stick to his idol of worship, however it brings only frustration, wretchedness, and misery.

Also, it should be remembered that such disillusionment is substantially more well-suited to deliver common negativity and worldly cynicism than it is to prompt spiritually insight and wisdom.

This same thing results at whatever point man sets his heart on anything short of, and other than, God. Augustine expressed: "By my very own sin Thou didst justly punish me. For Thou hast commanded, and so it is, that every inordinate affection should be its very own punishment" (The Confessions, Augustine, 1997).

Only God gives ultimate satisfaction and fulfillment. Man may set his heart on pleasure, riches, personal ambition, even family, nation, or companions. None of these can replace God. Whatever else put in the place of preeminent warmth and regard that properly has a place with God turns into an idol and will let one down in the end.

Man was made for God and can find life and fulfillment in nothing other than God.

Sin Disrupts Social Relations

3. As OFFICIALLY EXPRESSED, sin is against God and estranges or alienates man from God. In any case, while sin is basically against God, it additionally perverts and disrupts every one of the relations of man with man. These social relations are intended to be a blessing to man and are, except as they perverted. Man finds in these relations a significant part of the joy and blessedness of life. Truth be told, outside of these relations nothing resembling a human life could be lived.

Dr. John Thomas Wylie

A normal human life depends, first, on right relations with God and, second, on right relations with man. If the theistic interpretation of the world is right, then, everything depends upon being right with God. Be that as it may, if a man isn't right with God, he can't be right anywhere. So the sin that perverts man's relations with God perverts his relations with his individual man and with the whole creation.

In like manner, we find that the first sin told about in the Bible after the fall of Adam and Eve was the homicide murder of Abel by his brother Cain. From that day to this, every single human relation and foundation have been under the scourge, the curse of sin the very relations and establishments that were intended to bless man have frequently proved a curse.

Then again, Paul teaches that man is reconciled to God through the cross of Jesus Christ and along these lines discovers harmony with God. But, more than that, he teaches that through this cross, Jew and Gentile are reconciled to one another, and Jesus Christ turns into the ground of harmony among man and man only as among man and God (Eph. 2:11 ff.). In Jesus Christ God is making another humanity by removing the threatening, the hostility and alienation that separates them.

This clarifies the relation among religion and morals in the instructing of Jesus Christ. Jesus has now and again been decreased to the role of a moral or ethical educator, but he never shown morals for the good of ethics. Jesus knew too much about man to believe that man could be made right with man basically by dealing with human relations alone.

He knew and encouraged that man's fundamental relation is with God, and that insofar as man isn't right with God he would never be made forever right with man. Endeavoring to set man right with his colleagues without first making him right with God would resemble treating a debilitated man for surface side effects when he is being eaten up by an interior malignant growth.

In the teaching of Jesus, ethics are grounded in religion and religion convey what needs be in ethics. Truly, it isn't ethics and religion; it is fairly religion that is in a general sense ethical in its inclination. In the teaching of Jesus, true religion is ethical, and ethics are grounded in religion.

Man can't be right with man without being right with God, and getting right with God incorporates getting right with man. The central principle of religion is love to God. The central principle of ethics is love to man. These are not two but rather one. Love to man is attached in affection to God. Love to God proves to be fruitful in affection to man.

Sin scourges man in his very own personality by estranging him from God and distorting his relations with his colleagues and reviling, perverting every single human foundation.

Sin Causes Suffering

4. ONE QUESTION THAT emerges here is with reference to the connection of natural evil or suffering to moral evil or sin. There can be no strict partition between the two. The refinement has been called attention to as being, as a rule, the qualification between that which man suffers and that which he inflicts.

One is forced upon man by the weakness and ailment of his own nature and by the disorders of the natural world with which his life is inseparably bound up. The other he is in responsible for as being the perversity of his own will.

To hold that there is no connection between the two would be an untenable position. That would cut up the world and obliterate its unity. We can't concur that our world is therefore isolated, divided. Two things that are so personally intertwined in life must bear some causal connection.

Nor could we be able to say that the connection is that transgression (sin) is the outgrowth or articulation of natural evil or human weakness. This is essentially the view previously talked about, that sin is human weakness or limitation. Without a doubt there is a close relation between man's physical and mental weaknesses and limitations as purely natural and quite a bit of his moral weakness and sin.

However, to make sin nothing but natural weakness or its consequence would negate the unmistakable clear voice of conscience and the plain lessons of the Scriptures. This would not explain sin; it would explain it away.

We know that much human suffering is specifically and in a roundabout way because of man's sin. Both the man who sins and others also suffer because of sins. The connection isn't in every case simple to follow, however regularly it is self-evident. If all the suffering of humanity

Dr. John Thomas Wylie

because of its own perversity were removed from the world's history, that history would be very extraordinary reading.

Here the connection is obvious to the point that we don't experience any difficulty following it. We can't generally follow the connection in detail, but the wide blueprints are plain.

Be that as it may, shouldn't something be said about the suffering because of the disorders of nature herself, the violent winds, floods, seismic tremors, volcanoes, and so forth? There is a sign in Genesis and different spots that there is a connection between natural evil and the sin of man.

In Genesis work or labor is to be a part of man's punishment. This does not imply that work or action all things considered is a part of the punishment, for man was to keep the garden even before the Fall. What's more, after redemption there is to be activity.

God's servants will serve him (Rev. 22:3). Heaven is to be the wrong place for inactivity. In any case, the way that man is to gain his bread in the perspiration of his temples shows that the component of troublesome work came in on account of sin (Gen. 3:19). At that point it is said that the earth should bear thistles and thorns for man (Gen. 3:18).

This might be taken as a specific statement demonstrating that natural evil all in all came as a result of man's transgression and as an outcome. Paul's announcement in Romans 8:18-22 may show that the whole physical universe is to be remodeled and restored as a part of God's redemptive plan (Cf. II Peter 3:13).

Some have concluded because the announcement in Genesis that there was no suffering, no creature dying, no natural evil of any kind in the world before man sinned. Be that as it may, this is a shaky position for a few reasons.

In any case, there is no reasonable teaching anywhere in the Bible such that all suffering, animal death, and all natural evil are the result of man's sin. This is fairly an inference from such statements as we find in Genesis 3:17-19, Romans 8:19-22, and II Peter 3:13.

These statements don't clearly and obviously teach the situation under thought. What's more, we should recognize the unmistakable teaching of Scripture and our very own derivations from some pretty much broad inferences of Scripture. Where the statements are not clear and unmistakable, it progresses toward becoming us to rehearse an unassuming store in our certifications.

At that point something else to recall is that regardless of whether one hold; that natural evil in entire or to some degree, is the outcome of man's sin, still it isn't important to hold that man's sin went before in the order of time the presence of natural evil in the world.

This order in which things come in the purpose of God isn't really the order in which they appear in the temporal order.

The confusion and characteristic unsettling influences of the world may have been intended, regardless of whether implied entirely as punishment or not, to help man to remember his very own transgression and need of redemption.

Maybe the disorder of the physical universe is planned as an impression of the turmoil of the moral universe. Unless we are going to hold to a form of dualism, or make the physical universe the essential factor of which the moral is simply a reflection, it appears that the physical is in point of purpose and intention a reflection of the moral and spiritual.

However this would not require the remaking of the physical world at the season of man's transgression, with an inversion of the laws of the physical world. The imperfections and disorders of the physical may have been of the nature of "anticipative outcomes."

God could have made the physical universe to correspond to the foreknown state of the moral world. If God couldn't do that, he didn't have as much foresight and power of weather that he know will come in the atmosphere in which he lives.

So the statement in Genesis (3:18) does not necessitate that thistles and thorns started to develop simply after man trespassed. It is not any more important to hold that thistles and thorns initially started to develop after man trespassed than it is to hold that God changed laws of the refraction of light after the flood with the goal that the rainbow should first appear.

For each case it is probable that the divine wisdom chose certain natural wonders as of now in existence as a sign to man. The historical backdrop of the natural world would show that animal death was operative before man showed up in the world, and there is no good reason for holding that the Scriptures teach differently.

Dr. John Thomas Wylie

But whatever might be said about natural evil in general as being in whole or in part due to man's sin, there is no doubt that particular types of enduring are now and again the immediate or roundabout aftereffect of man's transgression. Nor is there any good reason for denying that this suffering is of the nature of punishment for man's transgression.

Some of the time these underhanded outcomes go to the person who submits the sin; now and again they fall upon others. Such evil outcomes some of the time come as the aftereffect of the violation of moral or spiritual law.

The Old Testament particularly emphasizes that affliction and death as the shortness of life came because of sin and disobedience to God (Exod. 20:12; Prov. 3:1;10:27).

This can't be made an unyielding law-in any event not to the extent of saying that one's state of worldly prosperity is a dependable list to one's spiritual condition; i.e., that disaster is dependably a sign that one is a great sinner, or that flourishing is an indication of righteousness.

(See the Book of Job and John 9:1 ff.). Still the truth demonstrate that righteousness advances great well-being and thriving, both in the nation and the individual, and furthermore that sin will in general abbreviate life and bring despondency and trouble. Experience and perception likewise legitimize the end that specific evils frequently pursue immorality and sin.

To a restricted degree, at any rate, at that point, natural evil or suffering might be viewed as the punishment of transgression, or as a penalty for sin.

When we go to the principle of providence as identified with grace, we will see that suffering or natural evil fills another need in connection to sin; that is, it is utilized as a means under grace for the advancement of Christian character; it serves a redemptive end. This we know both from the lessons of the Scriptures and from Christian experience.

This is involved with the saying of Jesus about the visually impaired man (blind man) in the ninth chapter of John. He says in substance to the disciples that they will never comprehend suffering and misfortune inasmuch as they try to interpret these only as the infliction of penalty for sin; they should see them as related to God's benevolent purpose toward humanity.

Dr. John Thomas Wylie

We must recall that each phase of life is to be interpreted from the perspective of God's redemptive purpose in Jesus Christ. Law and penalty don't express the last word. They express a true word, but the last word is spoken by grace and truth as revealed in Jesus Christ.

There is a penal perspective to suffering or natural evil; but there is additionally a redemptive aspect. For the man who rejects grace, suffering is fundamentally punitive; for the redeemed man, it is basically remedial and disciplinary. For society all in all, in extent as sin rules, it is basically penal; as grace rules, it is redemptive.

We realize that the race has got a lot of its advancement, mental, social, and moral, by striving to overcome natural evil.

We said further back that sin is the perversion of the good. Something of a similar kind may apply even to suffering and natural evil in general. Suffering and death could have been a part of the natural order purely as natural.

In a perfect order they could have served a good purpose. This does not imply that within themselves they would have been good, yet they could have served good ends. Suffering, at that point, becomes evil with the except as the grace of God intercedes to bring good out of natural evil.

In a moral order uncorrupted by sin, suffering and natural evils may serve morally good ends. Sin perverts this order and natural evil turns into a curse instead of serving good closures. The grace of God introduces the principle of redemption into the working of the natural order and makes the entire natural order, including natural evil to work for redemptive ends.

Sin Brings Death

5. THERE ARE PLACES in the Bible where the penalty of transgression (sin) is summed up in "death." God said to Adam: "In the day that thou eatest thereof shalt thou shalt surely die" (Gen. 2:17). Paul stated: "The wages of sin is death" (Rom. 6:23). Discussing a profane life, he says: "The end of those things is death" (Rom. 6:21). He says again that the mind of the flesh is death" (Rom. 8:6). James says that transgression (sin) brings death (1:15).

The inquiry emerges regarding whether this incorporates physical death, or is the penalty here spoken of spiritual death? There are places in the Bible where death obviously means spiritual death; for example, when Jesus stated: "He that liveth and believeth on me will never die" (John 11:26). He absolutely does not imply that one who believes in him will never die physically.

However, now and again death includes physical death. This is absolutely so now and again in the language of Paul. This is evident in I Corinthians 15, where he talks about the resurrection over against death. He likewise means to include physical death in Romans 5 when he discusses the universal sway of death as the consequence of Adam's transgression. When the Scriptures speak of death as the penalty for sin, they don't mean either physical or spiritual death to the exclusion of the other, however they mean death as a totality, both physical and spiritual the death of the whole man. There may be places where one aspect is emphasized. but neither phase of death is excluded.

There is no vital irregularity between this interpretation of death as related to sin and the idea that death is a law of life in the natural world. The biblical writers were not composing natural history. They were not composing as researchers.

They were giving a spiritual interpretation of the realities of the world in which we live.

Death is a law of the natural world. This law of the natural world is seen by the biblical writers as meaning that there is a fundamental rupture in man's life in his relation with God.

Information exchanged in the former section about natural evil as related with sin will apply to a great extent to physical death, because death is the summation and consummation of natural evil.

We can sum the matter up, at that point, by saying that for the Christian physical death is primarily redemptive and disciplinary; for the unredeemed man it is penal.

THREE

God's Redemptive Purpose

(Election)

WE HAVE SEEN SOMETHING of the nature and ruin of man's sin. To think about all men as resting under the scourge or curse of sin would be an exasperating thought if that were all that we could see. In considering sin we found that it has significance only in relation to a holy God.

The fact that makes sin such a terrible reality is that it is against a God of holy love. Sin would not be what it is unless if it were sin against God, and against such a God; nor would it show up in its actual character unless if seen in contrast to him.

But if seeing sin in relation to God draws out the darkness of, or blackness of sin, then again, seeing a God of saving grace that saves. Paul brings out the differentiation in the character of the two in Ephesians 2:1 ff. In verses 1-3 he shows the terrible darkness or blackness of sin.

Then he says: "But God..." He then draws out the glorious character of God's grace that saves. Once in a while when we speak about man's sin, we at that point turn and say that men are not all bad, or that they are not as they might be. Be that as it may, Paul shows more greater wisdom.

He finds relief from the darkness of the picture in the God whose character makes the blackness of sin so dark. Our refuge from the despair of sin isn't in any goodness found in man, nor in any power of man to save, but in God against whom man has sinned. Man's only hope lies in the goodness of the God against whom he has sinned.

Background Of the Doctrine Of Election

WHAT ONE BELIEVES ABOUT God's purpose as identified with our salvation will probably depend, to some degree at any least, on what he believes about some other things.

What's one's opinion about God? What's his opinion about the universe and about its relation to God? Who and what is man? What is his place in the universe and what is his relation to God?

It is apparent that what one supposes about such inquiries as these will determine what he supposes about election. Here as wherever else in religion the extremely imperative question is what one the thinks about God. What one believes about God will largely determine what he believes about everything else.

Consider a few inquiries that will have a particular bearing on this problem of election.

1. In any case, we are to remember that God is personal and purposive.

Obviously, if one thinks God an impersonal rule or power in or over the universe, he won't put stock in anything like election. Neither will he put stock in some other purposive action on God's part. All things considered, the Power that we call "God" may effect a few outcomes (they could hardly be called ends or purposes) that will prove helpful to man, but they could scarcely be considered as having been intended or purposed as useful (beneficial). They simply end up being beneficial by chance or destiny or somehow or another that we don't understand.

In any case, it was not so that that Jesus and Paul-the whole Bible, in truth regarded God. Plainly they regarded him as personal in a very definite sense and as working out explicit purposes in the world. Jesus regarded himself as having a specific mission throughout everyday life.

He regarded himself as having been sent of God into the world on such a mission. Paul's whole life was revolutionized and ruled by such a conviction concerning himself. That such was the conviction of Jesus and Paul is hardly questionable based on what we find in the New Testament.

One has a perfect right to differ with the New Testament on this issue. However, it is entirely questionable whether a man would have a right to regard God as simply the tendency toward integration, or something of that sort, and call that the Christian doctrine of God.

The Christian conception of God is unquestionably that God is personal and purposive. The whole Bible supports such a perspective of God, and so does Christian experience. Particularly is this true in the experience of a man who has felt the call of God to some specific form of Christian service.

In that respect the experiences of Jesus and Paul go through the lives of thousands in Christian history and in the present day. If some present-day rocker philosopher denies that he has had such an experience, the straightforward answer is that no one said that he had.

Dr. John Thomas Wylie

In any case, that is no confirmation that no one else has. If the objector says that no one can have such an experience, the appropriate response is that his denial can't balance the positive testimony of thousands of good and dependable people that they have had such an experience and that they have found the key to the significance of their lives in the experience.

2. In the second place, the historical world order is the scene of the working out of a plan of God.

If someone needs a scientific exhibition this is true, there is only one answer; to be specific, that no such show can be given. This doesn't involve scientific exhibit; it involves faith. From a scientific perspective, one may review all natural and human history and not be able to establish any conclusion of this kind.

Some such conclusion, be that as it may, is a need for a theistic perspective of the world. If there is a God who is the Creator and Sustainer of all things, then it definitely pursues that he created and Sustains the world for purposes of his own and that the world is the scene for the effecting of his purpose.

Some such assumption was plainly in the minds of the biblical writers. In Genesis 1:31 the writer says that God saw all that he had made, and, behold, it was very good. Clearly the author means that, with reference to the ends or purposes that the Creator had in mind for the world and for man, they were well adapted to carry out his purposes.

Otherwise expressed, in the finite and historical order the infinite and eternal God is becoming immanent for purposes of his own. This does not imply that there are in the historical order no elements that oppose his purposes.

The Genesis account demonstrates that there are such elements. So does universal human experience. In any case, the claim of faith is that this purpose will be carried out in spite of these intractable elements. Truth be told, the presence of these intractable elements helps to stress the necessity for carrying out such a purpose on God's part.

3. In the third place, Christian faith holds that God is working out through Jesus Christ and his church a redemptive program in the world.

This is to be join together with what has quite recently been said. Creation and redemption form one plan with God. Creation was for redemptive ends. Redemption was not hindsight on God's part. He didn't make the world, and unexpected to him have his plan destroyed by sin, and go to work to salvage something out of the disaster.

His was a unified plan from the earliest starting point. Creation looked toward redemption, and redemption is to be the objective and climax of creation. In Romans 8:18 ff. Paul seems to show that, in the consummation of redemption, the creative order comes to the acknowledgment of a teleology immanent within that order.

Supraiapsarian Calvinism was right in the sense that there was nothing deeper in the mind and purpose of God than his purpose to redeem.

4. A fourth thing to remember is that the processes and powers of both nature and history lie open to God's mind and are under his control.

As recently expressed, this isn't to deny that there are certain forces, particularly in man's will, that can and do oppose God and his purposes. Be that as it may, with reference to these, one of the Catch 22s of faith is that God works out his purpose regardless of the opposing forces on the world, and often through them.

We may take two occurrences in which this mystery is exemplified. One is the history of Israel. God chose Abraham and his relatives for an overall mission. In Abraham and his seed every one of the countries of the earth were to be blessed.

Be that as it may, Abraham's relatives overlooked this. They disavowed their overall mission. They turned out to be so completely focused in themselves that they overlooked the world beyond. They didn't feel that they had any mission to the Gentile world. They considered that God had chosen them for their own sakes and not for the world.

In any case, in spite of Israel's renouncement of her overall mission and obligation, and through Israel's rejection of her Messiah, God brought another religious order that is truly universal in principle. All the nationalistic and constraining elements were sloughed off, and Christianity supplanted Judaism.

The only completely spiritual and widespread conception of God and of worship that the world has known in this way appeared. Through Israel's disappointment God succeeded.

Dr. John Thomas Wylie

The other occurrence is just another phase of this one. Jesus Christ came to save. But, his people to whom he came rejected him. His own received him not. In any case, it was through their repudiation and rejection of him that he completed his redemptive work.

With wicked hands men crucified him, but in doing as such they carried out what was in the determinate counsel and foreknowledge of God (Acts 2:23).

This proposes where one of the most keen issues is attracted respect to this issue. Does God foreknow all things, including the free acts of men, even their most mischievous and insidious deeds? This has been the standard theistic and Christian position, even the situation of the individuals who did not hold to any distinct convention of decision and fate. Yet, a few men today deny that God's foreknows man's free acts.

This is the position taken by Dr. A. E. Garvie in his absorbing book, The Christian Doctrine of the Godhead. He rejects both foreordination and foreknowledge on God's part. This, he considers, is essential if man is to be free. He says that nobody can consider how an act could be both foreknown and free.

The outcomes of denying foreknowledge with respect to God are very serious. Dr. Garvie says that, however God know the breaking points inside which man's acts may affect the fulfillment of his purpose and he realizes his very own resources to meet the crisis.

In any case, the denial that God foreknows the free acts of man doesn't involve shallow confinement. If God does not foreknow the free acts of man, for every single pragmatic reason, he doesn't foreknow the future for man. If you remove the life of man, there is no future for the world.

Only to a balanced being do past, present, and future mean anything. And all development in time is to a great extent determined by the decisions and innovative exercises of men. If such decisions and exercises of men can't be known by God until after they have occurred, that, in actuality, leaves God trailing the parade instead of leading it.

Men have naturally trusted that some way or another God practice an opportune power over the undertakings of men. Be that as it may, providence means to see before. If God can't foreknow the free acts of men, nonetheless, his power of providence

Dr. John Thomas Wylie

is only a extremely diminished one. He can see ahead truth be told, unclearly. Thus his control of things to come would be very questionable.

This without a doubt isn't the perspective of either the Old or New Testament. This is manifest to the point that it seems to be unnecessary to contend the point. As per this disavowal, God himself did not foreknow the crucifixion and betrayal of Jesus. Jesus says, talking about the end, that nobody, not by any means the angels in paradise, neither the Son, knows, but the Father (Mark 13:32).

In any case, as indicated by Dr. Garvie Jesus ought to have included that not by any means the Father knows. In the event that he doesn't foreknow the free acts of millions of men going before the end, it is barely not out of the ordinary that he foreknows the season of the end. Obviously Jesus trusted that he did.

In addition, the position that foreknowledge on God's part excludes freedom on man's part is wholly gratuitous. Upon the day of Pentecost, Peter puts one next to the other the way that Jesus was delivered in the counsel and foreknowledge of God and that men slew him with wicked hands (Acts 2:23). A great many instances could be found in both Old and New Testaments where such issues are treated in the same way.

Another example was that of Paul while in transit to Rome to be tried before Caesar. They were caught in a great tempest on the Mediterranean and it appeared that they would all be annihilated. Amidst the tempest Paul was given assurance from God that he and the whole company would be saved (Acts 27:21 ff.).

However, somewhat later, when they were stranded on the shore of Melita, Paul told the military captain that, if the mariners were permitted to escape in the rafts, they would every one of (the detainees and troopers) die. So in Paul's mind the issue was sure or settled from the awesome perspective but then unforeseen so far as man was concerned.

By what means can a thing be settled or sure in God's mind and unforeseen so far as man is concerned? No man can tell. In any case, that does not imply that it can't be. We should remember that the infinite mind of God may have methods for knowing that transcend above the task of our limited minds.

The entire temporal order, including man and every one of his exercises, is grounded in the will of God. That involves a certainty of relationship between man's mind and God that is altogether not quite the same as anything known in human experience.

So we shall talk about election on the assumption that all of the events of the world order are known to God and that its forces are under his control. In the event that this be not really, obviously, to discuss election would be out of order. Be that as it may, we reject the assumption of the individuals who deny his foreknowledge and his power. `

5. For a right approach to the doctrine of God's purpose as related to our salvation, we help ourselves to remember something else; to be specific, that this doctrine as presented in the Scriptures isn't proposed as the solution of a scholarly conundrum; it is somewhat set out as a declaration of praise to God for his grace in saving us.

At the point when Jesus gets himself and his message detested and rejected, he says; "I thank thee, Father, Lord of heaven and earth, that thou didst hide these things from the wise and understanding, and didst reveal them unto babes" (Matt. 11:25).

At that point he adds: "For so it was well-pleasing in thy sight" Paul starts the Epistle to the Ephesians on the note of praise: "Blessed be the God and Father of our Lord Jesus Christ" (Eph. 1:3). He Blesses God since he blessed us with every spiritual blessing in Christ Jesus, and this he did as per the way that he chose us in him before the foundation of the world.

In Romans 8:28 Paul gives us that superb explanation that all things work together for good to those who love God. In any case, he proceeds to ground this in the way that he foreknew us and predestinated us to be conformed with the image of his Son.

It is in the climate of adoring acclaim for his goodness that we consider the thought set out in the New Testament, not in the atmosphere of theoretical interest. The doctrine dependably becomes a perilous thing when considered in any spirit other than that of humble praise to God for his grace that saves.

Election is a doctrine for the elect. It is intended to appreciate, cherish in them the spirit of humility and praise. For other people, it cherishes the spirit of haughtiness and restrictiveness. In the event that it does develop such a spirit in one, he in this way demonstrates he isn't of the elect.

If one becomes puffed up proudly over being of the elect, he accordingly demonstrates that he doesn't have a place with the elect. Election is intended to underline the way that God saves vulnerable sinners as a matter of grace on his part. It isn't meant as a speculative interpretation on a rational basis of God's activity among men.

God's Purpose In Its Racial Aspects

WE SHALL FIRST SEE God's purpose of redemption in its progressively broad viewpoints. We have perceived how the race as a whole fell under condemnation and death. Is there any proof that, with reference to humankind in general, God is working out a purpose? We believe there is.

The Religious History Of Man

I. THE GENERAL RELIGIOUS history of man would show that God has planted in man a voracious hunger for God with the goal that man can never rest until the point that he rests in God. Man's whole religious history is a record of man's search for God. In any case, this search for God is the result of a disposition that God has embedded in man's spirit. Definitely this pursuit isn't all in vain, and man's religious history is moving some whither.

The Old Testament

2. WE GET CLEAR signs of a redemptive reason for God in Old Testament teaching and history. When man trespassed (sinned), there was a glimmer of light that broke through the lowering clouds as a promise to the woman-a promise that has its fulfillment only in Christ (Gen. 3:15).

There was likewise a bow of promise that lit the obliteration of the flood with its light of hope (Gen. 9:9-17). The call of Abraham denotes another period in the advancement of God's purpose of grace (Gen. 12:1 ff.). God entered into a covenant with Abraham and his relatives by which they were made his exceptional people for an great purpose in the world.

They were not made his people, be that as it may, to the exclusion of alternate countries. They were fairly to be a blessing to other countries (Gen. 12:2,3). Israel was to be Jehovah's missionary to the countries (Isa. 42:1 ff.). Israel, be that as it may, as a country misjudged her main mission. She interpreted her call as meaning the avoidance of other countries, and, in this way, she wound up proud and egotistical in her spirit.

However it is the Catch 22 of history that Israel did not come up short, in light of the fact that out of her came the Redeemer, the one through whom God's redemptive purpose ought to be cultivated and who is, in this way, the fulfillment of every one of that was associated with God's optimal for national Israel. Old Testament history and teaching moved to their purpose and goal in Jesus Christ.

We get clear signs of a redemptive reason for God in Old Testament teaching and history. When man trespassed (sinned), there was a glimmer of light that broke through the lowering clouds as a promise to the woman-a promise that has its fulfillment only in Christ (Gen. 3:15).

There was likewise a bow of promise that lit the obliteration of the flood with its light of hope (Gen. 9:9-17). The call of Abraham denotes another period in the advancement of God's purpose of grace (Gen. 12:1 ff.). God entered into a covenant with Abraham and his relatives by which they were made his exceptional people for a great purpose in the world.

They were not made his people, be that as it may, to the exclusion of alternate countries. They were fairly to be a blessing to other countries (Gen. 12:2,3). Israel was to be Jehovah's missionary to the countries (Isa. 42:1 ff.). Israel, be that as it may, as a country misjudged her main mission. She interpreted her call as meaning the avoidance of other countries, and, in this way, she wound up proud and egotistical in her spirit.

However it is the Catch 22 of history that Israel did not come up short, in light of the fact that out of her came the Redeemer, the one through whom God's redemptive purpose ought to be cultivated and who is, in this way, the fulfillment of every one of that was associated with God's optimal for national Israel. Old Testament history and teaching moved to their purpose and goal in Jesus Christ.

Christa And The New Testament

3. BEGINNING WITH CHRIST, we have additional proof of a worldwide purpose for God. We have the proof of this in the principle of the kingdom of God in the New Testament. That kingdom was started with the coming and work of Christ (Matt. 3:2; Mark 1:15). He tells that the kingdom that started in such immaterial littleness is to end up a powerful undertaking (Matt. 13:31-33).

Many will originate from all directions (Gentiles) and will take a seat with Abraham, Isaac, and Jacob in the kingdom while the children of the kingdom (Jews) will be thrown out (Matt. 8:11,12). The matured Simeon welcomes the babe Jesus as the person who should bring a salvation which God had prepared before the essence of all peoples.

He was to be a light for revelation to the Gentiles just as the glory of Israel (Luke 2:31,32). Jesus commands that his gospel be preached to all countries (Matt. 28:19; Luke 24:47; Acts 1:8).

The book of Acts describes how the gospel got through Jewish limits and started to lay hold on the Gentile world.

Paul carried the gospel to the exact focus, even to Rome. Others had even gone before him there, for there was a congregation (church) in Rome before Paul went there. It is clarified in Acts that the proclaiming of the word to Gentiles was done under heavenly guidance. Paul went to the Gentile world under a unique call from God (Acts 13:1 ff., and numerous different sections).

Revelation gives us a realistic picture, for the most part in emblematic dialect, of the last and complete triumph of God's kingdom. The battle is long and hard, however complete and final triumph comes finally with the coming of the New Jerusalem down to earth from God.

God's Purpose As Related To The Salvation Of The Individual

THE SCRIPTURES TEACH NOT only that God has a general arrangement that is being done in mankind's history, yet in addition that God's purpose applies to the person. At the point when a man is saved, he isn't saved as an issue of chance or mishap or destiny; he is saved in pursuance of an eternal purpose of God. God saves men because he intends to. He saves a specific man, at a specific time, under a given situation, because he intends to.

Election does not imply that God founded a general arrangement of salvation and proclaimed that whosoever would should be saved and thusly, the man who wills to be saved is chosen in that he brings himself within the scope of God's plan.

The facts confirm that God has proclaimed that whosoever will be saved; but election is something more explicit and individual than that. It implies that God has announced to bring some, upon whom his heart has been eternally set, who are the objects of his eternal love, to faith in Jesus as Savior.

The general importance of the doctrine of election may be summed up in two explanations. The incarnation and cross of Christ imply that God wound up inherent in a corrupt, sinful race to found a kingdom of redemption. Election implies that of his own free grace, God turns out to be redemptively innate in the life of an individual heathen, and that he does as such deliberately. This precept may be investigated and abridged as pursues:

1. In the first place, when a sinner repents of his sins and believes in Christ to the saving of his soul, he does as such in light of the fact that God has brought him to do as such.

Men don't abandon sin to God all alone. God must move them to do as such if at any point they turn. This incorporates every single great influence, all gospel offices, all circumstances of environment, every single inner dispositions and promptings of heart and conscience that go into one's choice.

It incorporates the entire historical order in which one is so arranged as to have gospel privileges, and this order is seen as being providential. Particularly does in incorporate the internal promptings and leadings of the Holy Spirit.

To regard one's conversion from sin to Jesus Christ as the work of god is the unconstrained drive of the Christian heart. At the point when a Christian knows about somebody's abandoning sin, the primary articulation to go to his lips is, "Express gratitude toward God." But if is this not the work of God, he ought not be said thanks to. This is the perspective of Scripture as well as the unconstrained motivations of the Christian heart.

In the Bible salvation is everywhere ascribed to God. To save is the work of God. In any case, to save incorporates bring about this change of mind and heart that we call conversion. It isn't true that the sinner within and of himself repents and believes and afterward God comes into the procedure in forgiveness. No, God was in the process from the first.

He works to produce repentance and faith. He works to produce the conditions whereupon he can forgive. He seeks the sinner. We yield to a God who draws us to himself. We seek him because he first sought us. The good news of Jesus Christ is the good news of a seeking God.

He seeks worshipers (John 4:23). The Son of man came to seek and to save the lost (Luke 19:10). The seeking for of the Son of man is a revelation of the heart of God. Drawing men to Jesus Christ is the work of God. Without this drawing power men can't come to Christ (John 6:44).

Paul discusses God as calling men (Rom. 8:28-30; I Cor. 1:24;, and so forth.). By this calling he appears to mean more than a general invitation to men to be saved by the grace of God.

Paul's use of the term appears to relate rather to what Jesus discusses as the drawing of God in John 6:44. It is a dealing of God with the hearts of men that results in their coming to Jesus Christ and being saved. This effective call does not go to all, not even to all who hear the gospel.

Some are called; to them the gospel is the power of God. To others the gospel is a hindrance or silliness, even foolishness (I Cor. 1:23). This call gives one a spiritual personality that empowers him to get an insight into the meaning of the cross.

This drawing power of God is necessary, since man's regular tendencies are so contradicted to and opposed to God and righteousness that without it man will not come to God. Paul reveals to us that the carnal mind is enmity against God. It isn't subject to the law of God. Its nature such that it can't be (Rom. 8:7).

Man must be born again, since that which is born of the flesh is flesh (John 3:6). Thus one must die to sin (Rom. 6:2). The old man must be crucified (Rom. 6:6). One must deny himself and take up the cross to be a disciple of Jesus (Matt. 16:24).

2. In the second place, what God hence does in bringing men to himself and in forgiving and saving them, he does in pursuance of an eternal purpose.

He doesn't abruptly decide to save. From all eternity he has moved toward saving men. Every one of his activities in creation, in preservation, and in providence have led toward redemption. Redemption has been in the heart of God's purpose and action from before the foundation of the world.

Election is affirming the self-consistency of God. It says that God's nature, purpose, and activity are in conformity with each other. It is God's nature to redeem. The incarnation and cross of Christ came from the very heart of God. Additionally, it is God's purpose to save. His nature and his will are one, and both are redemptive.

What God does in time is the revelation of what God is in his eternal being. His nature and purpose for existing are objectified in his redemptive activity. Election is attesting both the self-consistency and the unchangeableness of God.

God may and does initiates new lines of action. He may get things done in the world or in the life of a person that he has not done previously, but rather he doesn't do what he had not considered or purposed. To deny election is to affirm that, when God saves a man, he does as such without having planned to do as such.

If God can do nothing new, if he is unchangeable as in he never starts anything new, God is the captive of his own immutability and his immutability, as Dr. Mullins(1959) says, would mean his fixed status. All things considered, God would be an impersonal principle or power without the capacity to go about as a person.

.

Then again, if God saves any individual without having wanted to do as such, he acts hastily, without purposeful premonition. The savvies movement among men is what is most cautiously arranged.

To state that election would be a self-assertive thing is to state that arranged action is self-assertive action. This is somewhat the inverse of truth. Movement that is arranged by an insightful personality has minimal component of discretion in it; action that is arranged by an omniscient personality has no assertion in it.

If election implies that God's movement in time is grounded in God's purpose in eternity, at that point it implies that in planning our salvation, he considered every one of the variables that went into the genuine circumstance. Election does not imply that God discretionarily picked this man and that one and disregarded this one and that one.

It implies rather that, foreseeing the man and his all out condition and circumstance, considering every one of the components that go into the creation of the man and his circumstance, God out of his own goodness planned to save him. He planned all the good impacts and every one of the means that accomplished the end. With this clarification of what election implies, the only way that one could keep up that election was a subjective purpose of God, is keep up that God saves individuals in a discretionary way. In the event that there is nothing discretionary in his purpose to save him that way.

When God elects a man to salvation, does God consider the man's faith? As said above, God considers each figure entering the circumstance.

He doesn't elect a man to be saved separated from faith but through faith.

In any case, this does not imply that faith is the ground of election. Faith responds to grace, it captures grace it doesn't produce grace. Grace inspires faith, produces faith. Faith is consciousness that we don't deserve salvation; it repudiates all claim on God and his grace.

Yet, while faith renounces all case on God and his grace, it embraces God and his grace and rests in his goodness. Grace goes before faith and is the ground of faith. Election is of grace; it is to faith.

Shouldn't something be said about reprobation? Is there a twofold fate? Does God pick some to eternal life and relegate others to everlasting death? God does not choose some for destruction in a same sense that he chooses some to eternal life. We may remember again that election is the working out in time of an eternal purpose of God.

Those whom God saves he saves in pursuance of an eternal purpose. In his genuine dealings with men in time, does God ignore some without saving them? To make that inquiry is to answer it. We should state that God passes over some without saving them, except if we will maintain that God saves all men.

The following inquiry, at that point, is this: Did God in time eternity intend to pass over those whom he really does pass over in time? Here again we should state that he did except if we will maintain an irregularity between God's purpose and God's activity.

If God's action is grounded in his purpose, all that God does he planned to do. If this isn't true, we would need to maintain that God did not know his own mind previously. He would be a changeable God. He would change on occasion in his action, as well as in his purpose or plan for men.

Be that as it may, another inquiry should be examined. When God passes over men and abandons them in their sins, does he have great ground for doing as such? The New Testament make this point unmistakablely clear). Men are casted off in view of their unbelief and their perversity in sin.

They are not cast off a role as an arbitrary matter, nor are they dismissed (rejected) on the grounds that God does not want to save them. The New Testament clarifies that God's love is for all men, that salvation has been accommodated for all, that we can earnestly offer salvation to all.

Man's very own unreasonable, perverse will is the main thing that keeps any one from being saved. God goes the extent that he can, reliably with his very own nature and with moral government of the world, to save any man and all men.

In managing men God has constrained himself by man's will, by man's sin, and by the moral order of the world. In a some regards God has made himself reliant on men. God is restricted by the material with which he deals and through which he works. God can't do simply anything. We are insisting right through this discussion that God is consistent with himself. He will not make a man a free and responsible specialist at then deal with him as a thing. To do as such would be the stature of irregularity on God's part.

God rejects men, then, only on the ground of their perversity, especially their unbelief. This implies God close out only the individuals who close themselves out. He won't forsee them to come in. He couldn't reliably do as such.

God predestinates to obliteration the those who won't be saved, and in that sense, he predestinates some to destruction. For their destruction the blame is on them, none on God. He can't save the individuals who won't be saved.

3. In the third place, then, we point out that election implies that all the credit for man's salvation has a place with God or belongs to God.

God steps up. God thought and planned before man did. God moves before man. Man yields and accepts what God plans and works.

Maybe there will even now be waiting in someone's mind the possibility that in the event that all the credit for salvation belongs to God, all the blame for the destruction of the lost is his also. This does not follow.

Paul says that God works all things after the counsel of his own will (Eph. 1:11). This is true as in the entire universe is under law to him, that all things and all men must operate as indicated by the techniques ordained by him, and at last will all add to his plan and purpose for the world.

In any sense, it isn't true that God specifically and proficiently produces all things. God does not work evil similarly that he produces the good. All the good (the morally good) known to mankind has its source and proficient cause in God.

He produces the good- all good. This isn't to deny that finite wills may need to work with him to deliver a few forms of good. However, it is to state that God and his will are the inspiring and guiding power in everything.

This is true in man's salvation. Salvation from start to finish is God's work. He plans, provides, and effects salvation. All credit for salvation is his.

Then again, the lost man is lost since he won't let God have his way. Where God has his way man is saved. Be that as it may, if the miscreant (sinner) won't yield, if he insists on turning God out of his life and on having his own way, at that point he is damned.

Giving God access to control (have his way) means salvation; closing God out methods mean punishment. In the event that the sinner closes God out, he can't reprimand (blame) God.

4. We need likewise to remember that God's purpose concerning any man incorporates, the man's salvation, as well as the good that God may do through him.

He chooses us for salvation, but in addition for administration (service). He has chosen and named us that we ought to go and prove to be fruitful (John 15:16). In Choosing us he had view for others as well as for us. He purposed beforehand acts of kindness (good works) that we should walk in them (Eph. 2:10).

We are chosen in Christ, Paul says (Eph. 1:4). He is the circle (or more correctly the sphere) inside which God considered us in ordaining us to everlasting life. It is only in him that God could think about us with any pleasure. In any case, in choosing us in Christ he had in mind as a priority for every one of us that union with Christ could mean to us and for us.

It implies salvation, holiness, service to God and man. All that God calls us to do in the world he had as a top priority in his mind for us in Christ when he destined us to be Christ's.

Objections To The Doctrine of Election

THE VAST MAJORITY OF the troubles and objections with reference to election develop out of misinterpretations of the doctrine and hurried derivations from it. The response to the objections, in this way, will take the form chiefly of clearing up the challenges by adjusting the bogus translations of the doctrine and demonstrating that the hurried or hasty inferences are not appropriate ends (conclusions) from the doctrine.

At the end of the day, the best approach to answer the objections to the doctrine is to set forward the doctrine all the more completely and correctly.

1. One objection to this doctrine is that it makes God partial.

People regularly quote contrary to this doctrine Peter's adage that God is no respecter of person (Acts 10:34). But, in context, particularly whatever remains of Peter's sentence, clarifies that what Peter implied is that God does not accept a man since he is a Jew or reject him since he is a Gentile. God has respect to the condition of the heart as opposed to national or fake refinements in his dealings with men.

No doubt there is in the mind of the one making this objection the assumption that God is under commitment to offer equivalent benefits, opportunities, and endowments (blessings) on men. However, in actuality, God does not bestow endowments on men with reference to common blessings (natural gifts.

Men are not equivalent in looks, in physical or mental capacity, nor in moral and spiritual gifts. he provides for one five talents, to another two, to another one. The Spirit bestows his gifts on men, to every one severally as he will (I Cor. 12:11).

When one expresses gratitude to God that he was born in a Christian land or of Christian guardians, or for good well-being, he is perceiving the way that God has given him endowments that he has not given to numerous others. The same is true if he expresses gratitude to God for salvation. In any case, the objector may state that, so far as normal gifts are concerned, these could not be equivalent since they come to us through natural methods and in a social order that essentially makes a difference among men.

We answer, may not the same thing apply as to religious gifts and opportunities? These likewise are mediated to us through natural, social, historical means, and it may be as unimaginable or impossible for God to reduce men to a common dimension of privilege and blessings here as in the account of natural gifts.

Religious endowments themselves come at least any partly through natural means. To put all men on a level of privilege and blessings may require that God remove men from the natural, historical, social connections in which they live. So the fact that God bestows more blessings on a few men than on others doesn't imply that he is "halfway" in a subjective way.

One thing we can say is that God bestows more blessings on every one than he deserves. His endowments all stream to us out of his goodness and grace. What God is under obligation to do is, not bestow equal grace on all men, but rather that he do no injustice to any. It will be appeared in the following segment that he isn't unjust to any.

2. Another objection is that it is low (unjust) to the non-elect since it makes his salvation impossible.

If man can't come without the exceptional drawing power of the Spirit and this isn't given, then what reason is the miscreant (sinner) to fault? This, the objector says, would hold the sinner in responsible for not accomplishing something which he couldn't do.

Be that as it may, this objection misconceives the issue. It assumes that, if God deserves the credit for the salvation of the saved, he, consequently, is responsible for the judgment of the lost. This isn't true. The following things should be remembered:

It must be recalled that God does not put anything in the way of salvation of any man. He doesn't prevent the coming to any man. God wills not the death of any man, but rather desires that all should come to repentance (Ezek. 18:23-32; 33:11; I Tim. 2:3,4; II Peter 3:9).

The doctrine of election isn't in opposition to this but goes further. It says that, not only does God desire the salvation of all, he decidedly purposed the salvation of a few. He has good justifications for what he does. The way that God does not save all is proof that there are constraints (limitations) on God that establish adequate reason behind why he should not save all.

We can securely say that God does all that he can consistently with his very own nature, the nature of man, and the moral order of the world to save all men.

No shamefulness (injustice) is done any man. Whatever God does for him involves grace. God desires the salvation of all. He has given salvation to all in Christ. He gives each man the welcome (invitation) to salvation. He brings influences to bear him to bring him into the way of life.

All this is grace. In regards of these things the miscreant won't come, he has no one to fault but himself. Insofar as he is reluctant to get the grace that God offers him, he can't gripe since God does not give him more grace.

The sinner's powerlessness (inability) is a failure (inability) only insofar as the miscreant refuses to recognize his reliance on God. In the event that he need to come, he can come. The trouble is on his part, not on God's. The hindrance is in the sinner. The main trouble is in the delinquent's (sinner's) attitude toward God. For that frame of mind (attitude) he is responsible.

There are constraints put on God in the issue that keep him from carrying out his desire to see all men saved. Man's freedom and perversity have a lot to do with it. We would be safe in saying that whatever aspects of the circumstance God takes in account in saving men, then he took account in electing men to salvation.

If this be not true, God is inconsistent with himself. Maybe we commit a mistake in thinking about the issue as though God chose man to salvation as a confined individual, without reference to the moral and historical connections in which the man lives.

Clearly this is a mixed up thought. Whatever God's purpose concerning any man may be, that purpose must relate to him in the complete environment in which he lives.

He isn't elected simply as a detached person. He is elected as an individual from the race living in a certain moral and historical environment. God's purpose with reference to any man's life is a part of his purpose for the race.

It doesn't seem that one man is elected to salvation and another not, on the ground that the man elected is ethically more deserving than the one not elected. All men are under judgment. All are sinners. God's purpose to save any is a purpose for grace.

God purposes to condemn the sinner on the ground on which he does condemns him; to be specific, in light of the fact that the heathen's (sinner's) attitude is with the end goal that God can't reliably save him. God gives him over to his very own fate since he would not be saved.

In any case, it might be asked: Does not the way that God purposes to condemn one man in view of his foreknown unbelief, carry with it that he elected another due to his foreseen faith? No; Election implies more than that. It implies that God purposed to produce the faith that is the condition of salvation. There is no faith to predict with the exception of the faith which God produces. He doesn't produce man's unbelief. God deserves credit for man's faith; man deserves the fault for his unbelief.

There are a host of objections that speak against the doctrine of election but we merely wanted to state a few.

God purposes that a thing should be done, we ought to for that very reason attempt to see that it is finished. Furthermore, if God purposes that it should be done, that is our confirmation and assurance that we can do it and our consolation in doing it.

In the event that God calls me to preach (and he has), I have the confirmation that my work won't be futile. He will give me more fruit from my work. Wherever he guides me to work, I have the confirmation that he has a work there to do and I can do it with God's assistance. Paul's confirmation and assurance as he worked at Corinth was that the Lord would be with him and no man should hurt him while he toiled there (Acts 18:10).

We have seen that except if God stepped up (took the initiative) with regards to our salvation and attracted us to himself, no man would be saved. We have quite recently observed additionally that the doctrine of election is a consolation, and encouragement to us in doing Christian work in that it guarantees us that our work won't be in vain in the Lord.

Later on we will see that it is the premise of the doctrine of providence and of the security of the believer. Election is the basal thought in the doctrine of salvation by grace.

Chapter
FOUR

The Redemptive Work Of Jesus Christ

WE HAVE SEEN SOMETHING of the degree of transgression (sin) in humankind and the demolish fashioned by it. We have additionally considered God's purpose of grace, both with regards to the race and with regards to the person. This purpose of God to save finds its revelation and means of accomplishment in Jesus Christ.

Christ is our Savior. "Thou shalt call his name Jesus; for it is he that will save his people from their sins" (Matt. 1:21). "The Son of man came to seek and to save what was lost" (Luke 19:10). "Faithful is the saying, and deserving of all usual meaning, that Christ Jesus came into the world to save sinners" (I Tim.1:15).

One trouble in philosophical or theological talks of the saving work of Christ has been theoretical procedures of thought. One case of this is found in the utilization of the term atonement. Christ's work on the cross has typically been talked about under the heading, and scholars have implied by it what Christ did in his death to make possible our salvation.

One scholar has said that the making atoning work of Christ "was only Godward, and only removed all the obstructions in the way for God's pardon of the sinner" (Boyce, J. P., 2006). This is the meaning typically given this term. In any case, it is doubtful if this satisfactorily speaks to the perspective of what Christ accomplished for us on the cross.

The New Testament rather mulls over the issue from the point of view of the result accomplished in the genuine reconciliation of the sinner. Besides, the word atonement is definitely not a legitimate interpretation of any word found in the Greek New Testament.

Dr. Mullins cautions against such unique procedures of thought (Mullins, E. Y., 1959). He brings up that law has been considered as some vague abstraction that Christ fulfilled; that the thoughts of penalty and fury of God have been treated abstractly; that salvation has been seen as though it involved accounting; that the Persons of the Trinity have been set over against each other; that justice and mercy in God have been seen as in struggle with one another, without any end in sight. Dr. Mullins talks about this subject under the title of "The Saving Work Of Christ," as opposed to calling it atonement.

We will make little use, in this manner, of the term atonement. We think of it as better to utilize New Testament terms to express New Testament thoughts. Our purpose is to endeavor to unfold what we find expressly set out or inferred in the New Testament. We will utilize mostly New Testament terms to do this.

Both in the New Testament and in Christian history, the most particular image of Christ and his saving work is the cross. We will focus, at that point, our talk in this chapter around the cross. We intend to incorporate into the term all that Christ achieved by his death for our sake.

The Cross As A Deed Of Redemption

1. IN ANY CASE, it is clarified that Christ accomplished something on which man's salvation depended.

Our redemption was his accomplishment. This is shown by such proclamations as that of Jesus when he said that the Son of man came to give his life a ransom for many (Mark 10:45). Whatever else this may mean, it demonstrates that he accomplished something that was fundamental for our liberation from sin.

Another announcement is that of Paul when he says: "Christ redeemed us from the curse of the law, having become a curse for us" (Gal. 3:13). The accompanying citations from the book of Hebrews make this point unmistakably clear: (Christ) "entered in once for all into the holy place, having obtained eternal redemption" (Heb.9:12); "but now once at the end of the ages hath he been manifested to put away sin by the sacrifice of himself" (9:26); "By which will we have been sanctified through the offering of the body of Jesus Christ once for all" (10:10).

"be that as it may, he (Christ), when he had offered one sacrifice for sins for ever, sat down on the right hand of God" (10:12); "For by one offering he hath perfected for ever them that are sanctified (10:14). In Revelation we discover this dialect: "Unto him that loveth us, and loosed us from our sins by his blood" (1:5).

Other entries could be given, but these are adequate to demonstrate that the New Testament teaches that our salvation relied upon something that Christ did for us. Christ saves, and he saves by virtue of something that he achieved.

Our redemption was his accomplishment. He accomplished something that makes possible for us a new relationship to God.

It is clarified that Christ's work for us was a deed of redemption. He unrevealed the attitude of God toward us, but his saving work was more than that. He came to make known to us that God was good toward us, however his work was more than that.

It has in some cases been spoken to as though Christ saves us by revealing God's disposition toward us. It would be progressively exact to state that he revealed God's attitude by accomplishing redemption for us.

In Christ God himself participated in the contest on our side and accomplished something for us. In the farewell talk to his disciples, as given in John's Gospel, Jesus reveals to them that they will be left in a world of tribulation. Be that as it may, he stated: "Be of good cheer; I have overcome the world" (John 16:33). Most likely he was talking here prospectively. He contemplates the triumph of the cross.

Envisioning it by faith, he discusses it as officially cultivated (as already accomplish). To his vision it remains as a practiced certainty. At that point on the cross, he stated: "It is finished"; and John said that he gave up his spirit (John 19:30). Maybe it was at this point, as indicated by Luke, he stated: "Father, into thy hands I commend my spirit" (Luke 23:46).

Both John's record and Luke's appear to be expected to establish the impression that the act of surrendering his soul in death to God was a conscious act and the completion of a process or exchange paving the way to that moment.

Something was culminated, an undertaking had been done. At that point Jesus gave up his spirit. The term is the one utilized for the selling out of Jesus by Judas. It proposes right around a formal exchange in which a process is brought to a formal end.

He intentionally yielded himself in death to God. He yielded his life back to the Father who gave it.

There is an articulation utilized several times in the Acts and Epistles that concurs with this thought. It is said that Jesus sat down at God's right hand subsequent to completing a task. He sits at God's right hand authoritative as Lord of the universe. The promise of Jehovah to David has been fulfilled and David's Son presently is delegated as Christ and Lord (Acts 2:33 ff.; 5:31).

He is waiting for every one of his enemies will be put underneath his feet (Heb. 10:13). In any case, he was not situated there until a definite phase of his work was done. He sat down when he had made purification of sins (Heb. 1:3). When he had made one sacrifice for sins forever, he sat down on the right hand of God (Heb. 10:12).

The author emphasizes that it was one sacrifice forever, in light of the fact that he wants to impress the idea that one was sufficient. It was something finished. It was a assignment, a task finished.

From the days of early gnosticism down to the present there has been an inclination in Christian idea to deny the verifiable as the genuine in Christianity. The propensity has been to recognize Christianity with general and necessary standards of truth. Christianity would in this way be diminished to a form of idealistic philosophy, pretty much evident, and separable from the person and historical work of Jesus.

It was over against this inclination that the supposed Apostles' Creed accentuated historical facts of our religion. Jesus was conceived of a virgin, lived, died, became alive once again (rose from the dead). Those were not general certainties of philosophy; they were realities of history.

Furthermore, they are in accordance with the New Testament. The New Testament is no course reading of religious philosophy; it is as a matter of first importance a record of actualities (facts). The Ritschlian religious theology was right in emphasizing that Christianity was established on certainties or facts of history.

Concerning the redemptive work of Christ, this idealizing process has endeavored to distinguish the atonement with the eternal suffering of God. It has been summed up in the explanation that the cross of Christ did not make atonement, but rather revealed the atonement. Here is the equivalent slippery propensity to make Christianity an ethereal philosophy- an inclination that originated from Greek or Oriental influences and separate or divorce it from facts.

Christian theology can promptly concur that Jesus Christ and his cross uncover God's eternal love for man. Truth be told, it should and affirms this. It can't live without this affirmation. Christianity consists of Jesus Christ and what he did for men.

What he did involves certain actualities with their significance. But, theology is most importantly a practical discipline, not fundamentally a speculative one. Also, it must demand that we can't have the meaning separated from the facts. The redemptive significance of Christ and his mission lies as a matter of first importance in something that he did. It was a deed in time, but the Eternal came in the form as a Person and a deed that he performed.

2. Something else that turns out in the passages cited above, and in numerous others, is that it was the death of Christ that established his redemptive act.

It is significant that from the time of the great confession at Caesarea-Philippi Jesus laid great accentuation in teaching his disciples on his moving toward death. (See Matt. 16:21; 20:17-19; Mark 8:31; 9:31; 10:33; and so on.). Up to that time Jesus had been waiting for the followers (disciples) to recognize him as the Messiah and turn out to be firmly convinced of his Messiahship.

When they report their acceptance of him as Messiah, he turns his consideration then to showing them the sort of a Messiah that he was to be, to be specific, a suffering Messiah. Is it a mishap that such a large amount of the space of the Gospel records is taken up with the most recent seven day stretch of the life of Jesus, his death and resurrection?

He was executed as an evildoer, a malefactor, crucified between two robbers. In any case, his death of disgrace and shame is what the evangelists put the emphasis on as the peak of a life of glorious administration (service) to God and man. This was the goal toward which his whole life moved.

This was true in the thought of Jesus. He intentionally pushed toward the cross as the place where his mission of redemption should be brought to fulfillment (consummation). As he confronted the cross there appeared to be something that was urging him on.

After Peter's confession at Caesara-Philippi, Jesus began to show his disciples that it was necessary that the Son of man should suffer and die and be raised from the dead (Mark 8:31 ff.). Since the followers currently had it settled in their minds that he was the Messiah, Jesus is by all accounts mostly concerned in instructing them that his messianic mission must be completed by suffering and death.

From here on he comes back to this thought again and again (See Mark 8:31 ff.;9:31; 10:32 ff., and parallels). When Mark utilizes the imperfect tense to express the thought (9:31). Jesus continued saying to his disciples that the Son of man is sold out (betrayed) under the control of heathens (into the hands of sinners) and they will kill him. Amid this period it was the steady topic of his teaching.

Particularly educating is Mark's record in 10:32-38. They were on their way, going up to Jerusalem. Jesus was pushing on ahead. His disciples pursued, amazed and afraid. They couldn't comprehend his attitude and his lead, and he couldn't disclose it to them. He took a stab at, really expounding, and they couldn't get a handle on it. His spirit and theirs were far apart.

The record in Matthew pursues intently Mark's record in this period, however Luke's is by all accounts autonomous. Luke's record, in any case, fortifies the feeling that we get from Mark. Luke returns over and over to the possibility that Jesus is looking toward Jerusalem.

In his few references to the issue it is hard to tell whether he is talking concerning one adventure to Jerusalem or multiple. But, there is one thing that isn't hard to see; in particular, that Luke intends to reveal to us that through this time of his action Jesus is intentionally looking toward Jerusalem with the sureness that death anticipates him there.

He comprehends what going to Jerusalem implies; yet he faces Jerusalem with full assurance to go there and satisfy his mission. He is conscious that he can't satisfy his mission outside of Jerusalem and the unavoidable conflict that is bound to some there with the authorities and the death that must originate from this conflict. (Luke 9:51;13:22;17:11; 18:31;19:11, 28).

In this circumstance Jesus stated: "I have a baptism to be baptized with; and how am I straitened till it be accomplished!" (Luke 12:50). He was anticipating the cross as the consummation of his work.

He taught his disciples that the Son of man must suffer (Mark 8:31). He viewed his death as a need. It was not necessary in the sense that was a bit much as in he couldn't keep away from it. He said that he could approach his Father and he would send twelve legions of angels to deliver him

(Matt. 26:53). His death was a bit much as in he was the casualty of conditions which he couldn't control.

His death was essential in a higher sense - as in his mission couldn't be fulfilled without it. He must die in the sense that he couldn't do God's will without dying and for him to do God's will was more important than to stay away from death.

He prayed in the garden to be delivered from death, but only inside the will of God. He died rather than to deny (refuse) God's will.

From the get-go in the service of Jesus there are evidences that he was aware of the need of suffering to fulfill his mission. The Voice at his baptism stated: "Thou art my beloved Son, in thee I am well pleased" (Mark 1:11).

The latter part of this adage is taken from Isaiah 42:1. The sign, at that point, is that Jesus at his baptism is perceiving himself as the "Suffering Servant" of Isaiah.

Maybe he was there starting to see that distinguishing himself with this diverse horde of sinners that John was baptizing implied misery, suffering.

The initial segment of the statement distinguishes him as the messianic Son of God, the second, as the Suffering Servant. The temptations in the wilderness depend on the assumption that Jesus was aware (conscious of) of Messiahship and that the fulfillment of his messianic mission involved misery, suffering.

Aside from this assumption the temptations are without significance. This temptation to abstain suffering by taking the simple, easy and popular way proceeded with Jesus entirely through his ministry and went to its peak in Gethsemane. When Jesus early in his ministry went back to Nazareth, he went to the synagogue on the sabbath (Luke 4:16 ff.). When he read the Scriptures, he chose a passage from Isaiah (61:1,2) and read about the Servant of Jehovah.

He revealed (he told them) to them that this Scripture was being fulfilled before their eyes. In this way he distinguishes himself with the Suffering Servant of Isaiah. As we have seen, Jesus said on the cross: "It is finished" (John 19:30). His redemptive work in the aspect of suffering and death was now accomplished.

The Cross And The Person
Of Jesus Christ

UP UNTIL THIS POINT, our dialog has set out that our redemption was a limited accomplishment with respect to Jesus Christ, and that what accomplished our redemption was his death.

1. The Gospel Of The Son Of God

WE SWING NOW TO another thought: to be specific, that the person who in this way accomplished our salvation was Jesus Christ the Son of God. This is major to any thought of this issue. The good news of the New Testament is the good news of the Son of God.

We mean by this, not a gospel preached by the Son of God, but a gospel in which Jesus is the object of faith, not just one in which he is the subject. A few men have kept up that Jesus was the case of faith, that we are to have faith in God after his example. They state that Jesus was the first Christian. His mission, so we are told, was to educate by precept and example, that God loves men, that he is our Father, and that we should believe him as Jesus did. To be a Christian is to have faith in God after the example set by Jesus.

We don't propose to talk about this entire inquiry here. We do intend to state this does not give Jesus his legitimate place in the gospel. We keep up that in the good news of the New Testament Jesus is the object of faith, not just the exemplar of faith. Obviously he believed in God, worshiped God, prayed to God; however the New Testament additionally encourages that he sustained a relation to God that was more close and major than that, a relation that no different has ever kept up or can keep up.

He was the basic, model Son of God. His relation to God as Son was essential to every other part of his being and causative in relation to all aspects of his mission. We maintain that this is the position, not just of John and Paul, but rather likewise of the whole New Testament, and that it is essential to historic Christianity.

Paul talks about the Son of God, "who loved me, and surrendered himself for me" (Gal. 2:20). When we start to talk, at that point, of one who died to bring us redemption from transgression and its curse, it should be unmistakably comprehended that we are not looking at something done for us us by another mere man. Our salvation isn't work by man; it is work by God. It isn't man's accomplishment; it is God's.

Here is the particular feature of the New Testament good news of redemption. It's anything but a gospel that enlightens us regarding something accomplished for us by an incredible and great man, nor a gospel that motivates us to endeavor to throw off sin for ourselves. It is the uplifting news of something that God in Christ accomplished for us and offers us as his blessing, something to be received by man, not something to be accomplished by him.

The suffering of Jesus, then, was more than the suffering of a good man who endured through the opposition of men as he battled for truth and righteousness in the world. It was that. the New Testament abundantly witnesses to the fact that his suffering were excellent for us and that we ought to along these lines suffer after his example.

In any case, to state that is the full or even the principle criticalness of his sufferings would not be true. Jesus was in excess of a saint to a righteous cause. What is here and there called the example theory of the atonement fails.

This theory holds that Christ was only a man, an incredible, great religious educator and virtuoso. He died because of devotion to truth and duty. He surrendered his life as opposed to yield what he conceived to be his duty to God and man. We are saved, if we should utilize that term by any stretch of the imagination, by following his example. He was the first Christian.

He was primus inter pares. He was not different in kind from us. He was the subject however not the object of faith. We don't trust in him for salvation; we have faith in God after his example, as he went even to death confiding in God to take care of him. what we require isn't somebody to appease the blame of sin, but an inspiring example to invigorate us to be consistent with the most noteworthy and best we know.

That is the thing that Jesus does for us. It is in this sense, and this sense only, that he saves us.

Whatever else might be said of this theory, it isn't the Christian view with reference to Jesus and his saving work for us. Jesus is our example. We are urged to suffer after his example (See Peter 2:19 ff.). His spirit in this regard ought to be our own. We are to deny ourselves and take up the cross (Matt. 16:24).

In any case, this does not state full view with reference to Jesus and his redeeming work. We are not exclusively to pursue his example, we are to confide in him as Savior moreover. We are to obey him as Lord. He made requests upon men that would have been ridiculous if he were not the object of faith as well as the subject (Luke 14:33).

We are to shoulder the cross. The cross is to be the ethical dynamic of our lives. As he loved, so are we to love. Be that as it may, the cross can't be constrained by us, we can't love after the case of Jesus, except if the cross is in excess of a case for us, except if it is a redemptive power that delivers us from the servitude of transgression (sin).

Inasmuch as I in my moral awareness am oppressed by the feeling of blame and cognizance am subjugated by the feeling of blame and judgment, how might I pursue the case of the sinless Christ in his life of love and conciliatory death?

The cross can't be my example except if it is first my redemption. To be my example it must be more. This is true for the basic reason that I am a delinquent, a sinner. while Jesus was not a sinner. I should be made unique in relation to what I am essentially before I can imitate Jesus.

The redemptive value of the suffering of Jesus may very well turn on the inquiry with respect to his identity. Is it safe to say that he was the Christ of God or would he say he was just a man? Did he suffer as one man among numerous or did he suffer as the Lord Christ?

We won't get the Christian perspective of the work of Christ except if we get the Christian perspective of his person. His person and his work are indivisibly connected.

The individual is to be declared as far as what he does for men, and his work for men is to be comprehended in the light of his identity. If Jesus was just a good man, though the most astounding and best, his death had redemptive noteworthiness just as any good man's suffering and death may impact other men for good.

However, in the event that Jesus was the Christ of God, continuing a one of a kind relationship to God and man, at that point his passing may have additionally have remarkable noteworthiness for men in their relation with God. The New Testament does not present Jesus Christ as only an extraordinary and great man who died for a unique purpose. It presents him as a unique Person whose death had remarkable exceptional significance for man's relation with God. His death could have exceptional value for us because he was an excellent Person.

Incarnation And Atonement

THIS IMPLIES THE IDEAS of atonement and incarnation in Christianity stand or fall together? Whatever else might be said about Anselm's book, Cur Deus Homo? (1903, 2005) his contention in one regard was sound. He attempted to answer the inquiry, "Why God - Man?" That is, he was endeavoring to reveal to us why God moved toward becoming man in the Person of Christ.

His contention was that incarnation was necessary to atonement. No one but God could meet the circumstance brought about by man's transgression. If Christ's death was just that of a saint or martyr to truth and goodness, it has no saving significance for us. God became manifested (incarnated) in a human life that he may meet the circumstance brought about by man's sin.

At times the view is advanced that the incarnation, as opposed to the cross, is the focal point of Christianity. Christ, we are told, represents union of God and man. Man needs to locate his actual destiny in God, and Jesus Christ as the incarnation of God saves us by helping us to find our fate in God.

In this view the main function of Jesus Christ was to epitomize the union of God and man and to enable us to discover our unity with God. John and Paul have been differentiated here-John as focusing everything in the Incarnation, Paul in the cross.

This be that as it may, is a bogus differentiation. John centers everything in the incarnation, but he also discloses to us this incarnate One is the Lamb of God that takes away the sin of the world (1:29).

He was lifted up that men might won't perish, but that they may have eternal life (3:14,15). He lets us know in the First Epistle that the incarnate Son is the propitiation for our sins and for the sins of the whole world (1:2; 4:10). Paul amplifies the cross, however it is the cross of the incarnate One. With Paul the cross and the incarnation go together.

A passage in Hebrews 10:5 ff., "Sacrifice and offering thou wouldest not, but rather a body didst thou prepare for me," has been confused (misinterpreted). The author is giving the meaning of Psalm 40:6 ff. Then over against the statement that in burnt offerings and sacrifices sin God has no pleasure is put the statement: "Lo, I am come;...to do thy will, O my God."

This inference is drawn from this that counts was the coming to Christ in the incarnation and his doing the will of God in a life of ethical obedience. In any case, we read a little further we find that the doing of the will of God spoken about is the will of God by which we were "sanctified through the offering of the body of Christ once for all."

The complexity the author is making isn't the contrast between the incarnation and the ethical life of obedience on one side and Christ's dying for transgression (sin) on the other. The contrast the author is making between the Levitical sacrifices and offerings for transgression (sin) and the once-for-all-offering of himself by Jesus Christ.

The previous could not redeem from sin and were not pleasing to God; the latter was as per God's will and brought eternal redemption. This author, at that point, joins the incarnation and a redemptive sacrifice for sins, and knows nothing (unaware) of a incarnation separated from such a sacrificial death of Christ.

The incarnation known to New Testament Christianity, then, is the incarnation of a God of grace who came into mankind's history to identify himself with a sinful race for its salvation. That salvation couldn't be accomplished without a sacrificial deed of redemption. The cross of Christ represents that deed of reclamation.

Neither the incarnation nor the cross means anything for man's salvation apart from the other. In the New Testament the two go together. What God has joined, let not the speculative religious philosopher put asunder.

Bishop Westcott spoke of the possibility that God would have been incarnated in a human life, regardless of whether man had never trespassed. Man's actual fate, we are told, could just along these lines have been acknowledged (realized), for man can't understand himself apart from God.

We can promptly concur that only in union with God can man's actual destiny be realized; but concerning how that union would have been acknowledged in a sinless world we should leave enveloped with the silence that belongs to the realm of things that the Almighty has reserved to his very own wisdom.

Note: The matter of Christian theology is to examine and set out as precisely as conceivable, accurately as possible; how God saves men in this actual sinful world, not to speculate about what God would have done in a totally different kind of world.

The Cross And the Character Of God

IT SHOULD BE REMEMBERED that theology is concerned, first, last, and all the time, with the character of God. Entirely, theology is concerned with nothing else, except only how God saves men in a sinful world.

We come now, to the questions with respect to how the cross of Christ and the character of God are related. Indeed, even an easygoing associate with the historical backdrop of Christian thought will uncover to one that in theology these two thoughts have been essentially related.

What one accepts (believes) about God will figure out what he accepts (believes) about the cross. At any rate these two thoughts are crucially interrelated. What one accepts (believes) about either will help figure out what he accepts (believes) about the other.

What required the death of Christ? How does the cross of Christ save us? What did he achieve in his death by virtue of which we are saved?

In discussing the issue, we are expecting that the cross was a need. It was neither a mishap of history, something happening in a good for nothing world, nor a subjective arrangement of the divine will, We are assuming that there was a profound need in the moral universe for the cross.

Current theology has been divided over the inquiry with respect to whether this need for the cross lay in God or in man. Speculations (theories) of atonement have been divided on this line-some being classed as holding that the atonement was for satisfying God with reference to man's transgression (sin) and making it feasible for God to save man, different theories being classed as holding that this need for the cross lay in man and his demeanor toward God as opposed to in God and his attitude toward man. Whatever one keeps about this will go down eventually to what one accepts (believes) about moral nature of God.

The Moral Necessity For The Cross

In Relation To Sin

THE NEED FOR THE cross lay in the moral nature of God in relation to man's sin.

The cross of Christ was not intended to affect either God or man with the exception of as related with the other. It affects either God or man just as God is related with man or as man is related with God. It isn't true, along these lines, to state that the cross was intended to affect God but not man, or man but rather not God.

Either proclamation would be meaningless. We would concur that it was intended to affect God essentially given it is comprehended that we mean God in relation to man's salvation. All things considered it would make no difference to state that it didn't affect man. God is the primary factor in religion, but man is also involved with any issue touching religion.

To discuss anything as affecting God but not man is to say that it had nothing to do with religion or God's relation to man. Why talk about it, at that point?

God couldn't just disregard sin as though it didn't exist. Quite a bit of our present-day thought treats sin very daintily; it scarcely perceives a wonder such as this and even needs to dispose of the term. Such idea is set apart by moral shallowness. So far as it perceives sin, it will in general see it as a terrible dream-the faster one overlooks it the better.

Indeed, even some professedly Christian masterminds look on God as a decent normal Somebody (or Somewhat) who never holds anything against anyone. His fundamental concern is to keep everyone in a good humor with him and with every other person.

The God of the Bible is a God of moral earnestness. He can't slight or disregard sin. Nor would he be able to treat the righteous and the profane (unrighteous) alike. There is a necessary response of God as moral (or holy) against the sin of man. If God should simply disregard sin, he would not be an moral God. In the last examination, this would imply that transgression (sin) isn't sin. All things considered God would not be God and we would be living in a non-moral universe.

The inquiry emerges, at that point, concerning how God should deal with sin. If God can't slight, disregard sin, what can be done?

One possible thing that he may do, if he isn't to slight, disregard sin, is to distribute correct punishment to each individual sinner. That is, he could manage men on the place of correct retributive justice. This, in any case, would prohibit the likelihood of salvation.

On that plane, there could be no salvation. Each man would suffer the punishment of his own transgressions (sins), God's justice would be vindicated, and the whole human race would be left in its lost condition.

In God's Purpose To Save

OUR QUESTION MUST BE expressed a little more definitely. It isn't adequately characterized if we talk about the relation of God's character to sin. Before to we can grasp our concern, we should bring into the dialog the reality of God's purpose to save man.

We are not managing the problem of the cross until we see it as God's strategy for carrying out his purpose of redemption. Until we along these lines see the matter, we are dealing to a great extent in speculative deliberations, which is rarely a beneficial exercise in theology.

How does the cross of Christ save man?

Accepting the record as we have it in the New Testament, translated in the light of Christian experience and Christian history, we trust that specific things can be asserted. These thoughts, presumably, can't be viewed as a complete theory with reference to the redeeming work of Christ.

Maybe no such theory will ever be detailed. Surely none has up until this point. In any case, we can at any rate translate to ourselves a portion of the crucial moral substances involved with our salvation through the cross of Christ. This will add to our psychological confirmation and spiritual strength and fulfillment as Christians and will assist us with interpreting our religion to other people.

In dealing with the cross as related to the character of God, scholars (theologians) have normally thought about the redemptive work of Christ as related either to the righteousness (justice) or to the mercy of God. Some have seen the cross for the most part as an interest of God's justice and some as an outflow of God's love.

For all intents and purposes each man attempted to think about Christ's saving work in relation to both God's righteousness and his love, but a proper balance has generally not been maintained.

The Cross And The Righteousness Of God

The Cross As Vindication Of Righteousness

1. OUR CRUCIAL RECOMMENDATION here is that the cross vindicates the righteousness of God in our salvation.

We mean by this that the cross demonstrates that God saves us on principles of righteousness. The cross of Christ is the most uncompromising judgment of human sin to be found in either history or experience. Human selfishness and sin stand completely condemned before that cross as no place else in God's reality.

This judgment (condemnation) of man's sin in the cross isn't just man's judgment; it is God's judgment on man and his transgression (sin). This is clarified in the Gospel of John. In this Gospel, it is made plain that man's judgment of Christ turned into God's judgment on man.

It became God's judgment on the whole historical order to which we have a place, to which we belong. The cross condemns this order as a fallen order. God's judgment lays on it all in all. The whole world lies in the evil one and is condemned by the cross.

This historical order (all things considered) can't be redeemed. God can work out a program of redemption within this historical order and on the basis of it; however our American liberal theology that sees this historical order as only somewhat weak and as requiring just a touch of doctoring to be transformed into the kingdom of God is doomed to disappointment in view of the cross.

In the New Testament overall, the cross condemns the entire religious, civil, and social setup of the historical order of the world. The Christian isn't to love the world, neither the things in the world (I John 2:15). He isn't to lay

Dr. John Thomas Wylie

up treasures on this earth. In the event that he does, he is in danger of setting his heart on the earth and its treasures (Matt. 5:19 ff.). He is to be in the world, but not of it (John 17:14 ff.).

Redemptive Righteousness More Than Retributive Justice

2. The righteousness of God showed in the cross is of a higher sort than retributive justice. In some cases scholars (theologians) have differentiated righteousness in the sense of retributive justice with the adoration or mercy of God and have set them over against one another in sharp difference.

One scholar (theologian) said that mercy and justice are presented in the Scriptures "as opposing; mercy arguing for the sinner, and justice demanding his punishment" (Boyce, J. P., 2006). As indicated by along these lines of reviewing the issue, the cross of Christ is a sign of righteousness, in light of the fact that on the cross Christ satisfied the demands of justice in paying the penalty of our transgressions (sins).

Subsequently the cross was an indication of the relentless interest of heavenly equity that transgression be rebuffed. Not in any case the mercy of God could turn away the demand of justice that penalty for sin be demanded.

It appears to me, nonetheless, that as opposed to stating that the cross of Christ was the infliction of punishment on Christ for our sins and along these lines an exhibition of divine justice, it is smarter to state that it was a show of righteousness of a higher kind than retributive justice.

When sin is condemned in retribution, it is condemned without hope; it is a condemnation unto despair. When sin is condemned by the cross, it is condemned savingly: it is a condemnation that is charitable in its character and is the ground of hope.

The condemnation of wrongdoing (sin) in the cross is in excess of a presentation of retributive justice. It is a condemnation that becomes out of an exhibition of grace that saves. It results from a sign of the mercy of God toward the disgraceful. Retributive justice apportions to each man rewards and punishment as per his deserts; mercy manages men better than anything they merit or deserve.

Grace transcends law. The good news of Christ transcends above the law technique for managing sin. The law strategy for managing sin is the technique for retributive equity (justice). Penalty is executed against the delinquent (sinner). Righteousness as retributive justice is in this way showed and vindicated. Be that as it may, grace transcends above this technique.

Grace additionally shows and vindicates righteousness, but it is righteousness that transcends retributive justice. It is redemptive righteousness. Retributive justice vindicates itself in penalty; redemptive righteousness vindicates itself in the cross of Christ. Suffering under law is reformatory; Christ's suffering was redemptive.

The scholars (theologians) have been correct who recognized justice (or holiness, whatever term they may utilize) and grace or redemptive love. In any case, they have been off-base in making equity (holiness or righteousness in that sense) better than affection or grace and in translating them instead of one another. Equity was in this manner made the decision trait in God and love needed to bow to its demands.

The essayist heard a minister say that God never excuses sin; he may pardon the heathen, but the wrongdoing (sin) must be rebuffed (punished). This might be valid; yet on the off chance that so Jesus wasn't right. He talks over and over of God's forgiving sins, debt, trespasses, and so on., and he makes sin (debt or trespass) the immediate object of the action word and the miscreant the aberrant article.

This creation of justice preeminent will in general make our salvation something that God owed to Christ as an issue of debt. It likewise will in general remove the component of grace in God's dealings with us. All things considered, Christ would be gracious; God would be just. Christ purchased our salvation from God and made an endowment (gift) of it to us. Hence we would be committed to Christ however not to God.

It is extremely the other way around. Grace transcends above justice or law. It rises above the law strategy for managing man. Law was just an incomplete disclosure of God. Grace rises above law and takes its qualities up into itself. It is finished (fulfilled) in Christ.

Paul shows that this legalistic technique for managing man has been repealed. The mandates of the law were nailed to the cross (Col. 2:13 ff.).

There has never been a more noteworthy tragedy in theology than the understanding of Paul's doctrine of justification as legalistic. Paul isn't diminishing the gospel to a type of legalism. As Dr. Mullins brings up, he was fighting legalism.

The grace of God reveals a higher type of righteousness in God than does the law and requires a higher righteousness in man. What's more, what it calls for it produces. This is the reason that Jesus says that he doesn't revoke the law but fulfills it (Matt. 5:17). Paul says that faith fulfills the law (Rom. 3:31). (See additionally Rom. 6:1 ff.; 8:1 ff.). The thing which the law neglected to do grace achieves.

It produces righteous men. In any case, it is righteousness that rises above legalism. It has the component of grace in it. This is appeared by the teaching of Jesus that God won't forgive us if we don't forgive our kindred men (Matt. 6:12, 15, et al.).

Except if the grace of God delivers a benevolent (gracious) character in us, it doesn't do much for us. The righteousness of the gospel transcends legalistic justice; it is justice raised to the plane of grace.

The cross is the highest manifestation of the holiness of God, and holiness incorporates both the seriousness or justice of God and his mercy or grace. Grace isn't indifferent toward sin. It is love with the element of righteousness at its heart.

The mercy of God, at that point, manifested Christ does not imply that God loosens up the demands of the moral law and excuses men in their transgressions (sins). Nor does it imply that God merely relieves men from the punishment because of transgression (sin). Such an interpretation of mercy is the Mohammedian as opposed to the Christian understanding.

In the Mohammedan origination of mercy, God loosens up the demands of the moral law, and excuses those whom he accordingly supports (favors). It is God's technique for self-assertively discharging his top choices from the moral outcomes of their insidious deeds. No sort of a divine being (god) can do a wonder such as this with the exception of one who is a moral dictator. The God and Father of our Lord Jesus Christ isn't that sort of a God.

He isn't a discretionary tyrant, but a God of grace toward the wicked or sinful. In any case, grace isn't moral lack of interest nor moral laxity.

It is mercy, but mercy with moral integrity at its middle. It is love but it is holy love. It wills to save, but on standards of righteousness. Paul experienced considerable difficulties shielding men from translating the grace of God as significance such good lack of concern on God's part as would enable men to proceed in transgression (sin).

Two of the most powerful influential theories of atonement dealt with the issue from the point of view of vindicating the righteousness of God.

The Governmental Theory

ONE OF THESE, THE administrative hypothesis, translated Christ's death from the perspective of God's legislature of the universe. The hypothesis was figured by Grotius, A Dutch legal lawyer. It was put forward in expound frame in his treatise called The Satisfaction of Christ. He wrote in reply to Socinus, who denied that any fulfillment was essential as a state of the forgiveness of sins.

Grotius kept up that there was need for fulfillment (satisfaction). That need lay in God's legislature of the world. The fulfillment was not made to God as a private individual but rather as Governor of the world. So far as his very own advantages or nature were concerned, God could bear to pardon without fulfillment.

Be that as it may, God acted, not as a private individual, but rather as Governor of the world, and all things considered a Governor he should require fulfillment for the interests of good government. It was not God's temperament accordingly, but rather rectoral equity that requested fulfillment. The need for fulfillment lay in the way that, should God openly forgive without requiring fulfillment, sin would not be controlled legitimately and the interests of his ethical government would be jeopardized.

Grotius uninhibitedly utilized such terms as punishment and penalty in talking about the issue, but the fulfillment that he demanded was not the strict curse of penalty as normally comprehended or as put forward in the correctional hypothesis.

It was anything but a strict compensation exchange. It was somewhat the possibility that the death of Christ was such an appearance of God's dismay toward wrongdoing (sin) that God could forgive without empowering that he was indulgent toward transgression (sin). It represents an essential component of truth.

One of the incredible shortcomings is in viewing the ethical law as rather a discretionary authorization and a lot in deliberation from the ethical idea of God. The law is viewed as a lot as an unadulterated order of will instead of as an issue of moral need.

Henceforth the law was viewed as something that God could unwind voluntarily. The death of Christ was such an appearance of God's dismay toward transgression (sin) that God could securely forgive; that is, remit the penalty of the law.

The Penal Theory

Development And Meaning

1. THE OTHER THEORY that tries to decipher Christ's redeeming work from the outlook of God's righteouness nature is the penal theory. This theory isn't a work by any one man; it created over an impressive time frame. It is a genuine development from Anselm's view and is the legitimate beneficiary and successor to his view.

One of the principle contrasts is that Anselm said that it was the satisfaction of God's honor as irritated or offended by man's wrongdoing (sin) that required the death of Christ, while the reformatory (penal) theory says that the need for his death lay in the demands of God's justice in relation to sin.

The theory has received numerous common explanations in theological literature, some of them set forward with the incredible intelligent keenness and learning and some progressively prevalent and evangelistic in their intrigue. The theory has demanded the substitutionary part of Christ's work and has here and there carried this so far to endeavor to translate his substitution in quantitive terms.

This led in the stricter forms of Calvinism to the possibility of a restricted atonement. Now and then, in translating the issue under the similarity of an obligation (debt), it was said that it would not be just for God to collect the obligation (debt) from both Christ and the heathen (sinner). God, it appears, was nearly viewed as being under commitment to save the man for whom Christ died.

Weaknesses

2. It VERY WELL may be effectively perceived how this view now and again would in general present absolute opposite inside the Godhead, the Father being viewed as the epitome of justice requiring the heathen's (sinner's) punishment and the Son viewed as the encapsulation of mercy trying to save the delinquent (sinner).

No decent arrangement obviously ever very said that, however it was nearly suggested now and again. The view additionally - at any rate, in its progressively more rigorous structures - would in general run a line of cleavage between the justice of God and the mercy of God. So, as well as justice of God was looked on as fundamentally, if not solely, corrective (penal) in its nature, and was magnified to the incomparable place among the characteristics or attributes of God.

This was true, regardless of whether the term utilized was justice, righteousness, or holiness. The main characteristic for holiness (righteousness or justice) was its demand for allotting precise punishment to sin; and this must be done whatever else may happen.

God's main purpose came to be viewed as the distributing of rewards and punishments to the subjects of his ethical (moral) government as per their deserts. This was as per the accentuation on justice as the chief or preeminent characteristic of God.

It was regularly said that God may exercise mercy, but he should punish sin. Mercy on God's part was discretionary (optional), punishment was mandatory. This technique for interpreting God and redemption experienced difficulty with John's explanation that God is love (I John 4:8).

This theory, at that point, can scarcely be viewed as a sufficient interpretation of the redeeming work of Christ.

Every theory worked out has had a component of truth in it, however no complete theory has yet been propounded. The penal theory has been exposed to analysis, criticism for over a century. Its weaknesses have been called attention to, and its insufficiency uncovered.

While a considerable lot of the rivals of this theory have been found outside the ranks of outreaching Christianity (evangelical Christianity), many have also been found inside the ranks, and the theory in its progressively inflexible highlights or rigid features is illogical.

As officially called attention to, this theory will in general set the attributes of God over against one another in a ridiculous way, regardless of whether not to set the Persons of the Trinity contrary to each other. To view the suffering of Christ as the exacting installment of an obligation (debt), with the goal that it could be estimated in quantitative terms, is completely irrelevant.

To view sin as a strict obligation (debt) and the death of Christ as the exacting installment of an obligation is to literalize dialect that tries to set forward spiritual truth in the dialect of a similarity. A similar thing genuine that we look to translate the work of Christ as strict heading of penalty. As per the major principles of this hypothesis itself, penalty in that capacity vindicates justice and nothing more.

Penal suffering in this way, isn't redemptive in its nature. It couldn't save. It is thought of as dropping the guilt of past transgression (sin); but it doesn't accommodate the revolution of character nor outfit a sufficient dynamic for Christian living.

The cross of Christ as exhibited in the New Testament accomplishes more than drop the blame of past transgression; it is the unrivaled source and dynamic of the Christian life. It isn't one of the wellsprings of salvation and Christian living; it is the unrivaled source and intensity of salvation and the Christian life.

The cross of Christ stands, at that point, not for the uncovered perseverance of punishment. The rivals of this theory are maybe right when they demand that penalty (or guilt)) accordingly isn't transferable. If we mean by blame (guilt) individual sick desert, Christ was not liable. As Dr. Mullins (1959) says, he couldn't have borne penalty in the conventional sense of the term. He didn't suffer the personal displeasure to God's will and in his death he was executing the redemptive great joy of God for the benefit of man.

When he is spoken of to as coming to do God's will, it is God's will in making an offering for wrongdoing (sin) that he was executing (Heb. 10:5-15). His suffering were redemptive rather than penal.

Some of the time the idea of substitution has been conveyed to the point of insisting that Christ suffered in quality and quantity what the

Dr. John Thomas Wylie

redeemed would have suffered had Christ not redeemed them. Such a position can barely be defended.

It isn't irrational to feel that one component in the suffering of the unredeemed in the following life, just as in this, will be remorse subsequent to having given as long as he can remember in unbroken service to God and man and while dying in loyalty to God's will.

Most likely Jesus did die spiritually in the sense in which the heathen (sinner) does. Sin kills in that it isolates from God. Jesus did not die spiritually as the sinner does who drives God out of his life. Jesus died to sin (Rom. 6:10), by virtue of or for transgression (sin) (Gal.1:4), and for the sinner (Rom. 5:6,8), but he didn't die in sin and to God as a Sinner does. The punishment of sin as suffered by the remorseless is to be cut off from spiritual life in God. Jesus did not suffer penalty in that sense.

If We may utilize a similarity to toss light on the idea of the nature of suffering of Jesus for our sake, we may think about a criminal being executed for his wrongdoing (sin).

The suffering of Christ over us would be progressively similar to the suffering of the criminal's Christian mother as she would give her life for her child than the suffering of the solidified criminal himself.

The facts would demonstrate that his vocation of wrongdoing (sin) would have so solidified him that he would be unequipped for suffering as she would suffered. Her suffering would be more serious than his and of an different order.

In addition, the penal view will in general see God as having a great time suffering in that capacity. It looks on him as demanding such a great amount of suffering over so much sin. Suffering is of value only when related fundamentally to moral or spiritual ends. God isn't revealed in the New Testament as a vast Shylock demanding his pound of flesh before he will exercise mercy.

Strong Points

In any case, it had the advantage of giving an unmistakable and reasonable clarification of the need for Christ's death as related to the nature of God from one viewpoint and to man's salvation on the other. Since God as just will undoubtedly punish sin, the penalty must be borne with respect to the heathen or someone who took his place.

He could be saved only in the case that someone should penalty for him. Among the historic theories of atonement, it remains at the highest priority on the rundown, with regards to giving a sensible record of the need for Christ's death.

Once more, the theory is in a strong position in its intrigue to those Scriptures, in both the Old and New Testaments, that speak to the saving estimation of the sacrifices or of the blood of Christ as relying upon the idea of substitution or the vicarious component of the offering. Without a doubt that component of the sacrificial work of Christ is exhibited as of its very essence.

The ground for this is laid in the Old Testament sacrificial system. The saving work of Christ is spoken to as saving us from God's anger and in some genuine sense as propitiatory and substitutionary.

One of the incredible weaknesses of the example and moral perspectives was in sidestepping or denying this component from Christ's work. Indeed, even the governmental theory was frail now, despite the fact that in a more grounded position than these other two perspectives.

The third respect in which this view was strong was in its intrigue to the miscreant (sinner) who was under a sense of failure and guilt. A heathen (sinner) with an intense feeling of disappointment and blame needs a gospel that assures him that somebody has made sufficient arrangement for a free pardon for his transgressions (sins). Different theories were frail, weak, at this point.

While the penal theory misses the mark as an adequate record of Christ's redeeming work, we see that it stands for a few components of truth. Christ's work for us was genuinely substitutionary as in he took the scourge of death on himself that we may be saved.

He tasted death for every man (Heb. 2:9). He was made to be sin for us all that we may become the righteousness of God in him (II Cor. 5:21). He redeemed us from the curse of the law by being made a curse for us (Gal. 3:13). What was the curse of the law? Dr. Burton,(1909) makes it still progressively positive about what is implied by the scourge of the law. The law was a legalistic system which was a curse.

Dr. John Thomas Wylie

The revile was the scourge of imagining God after a legalistic mold as one who holds men to strict record for their wrongdoings. To be redeemed from the scourge of the law intends to go to a superior comprehension of God and understand that the law as a legalistic framework distorts God. He says: "From this it pursues further that redemption from the scourge of the law isn't forgiveness of sins, however redemption of the brain (deliverance of the mind from a misconception of God attitude towards man) from a confusion of God's disposition toward men" (Burton, 1909).

That is, the law in holding that God holds men to a strict record for their wrongdoings (sins) distorts God, and we are redeemed from the scourge of the law when we come to comprehend that this conception of God in relation to sin isn't true. Jesus, as well, at that point more likely than not misconceived God when he tells how strict an account men must give. He says that one who says to his sibling, "Thou fool," will be in danger of the hellfire of fire (Matt. 5:22).

Paul holds that Christ delivered us from the law as a legalistic framework. In any case, it is practically sure this isn't what he implies by the curse of the law. The curse was the curse of death. That curse went ahead us on account of our transgression (sin).

The law articulated that curse of death upon us in view of our inability, failure to satisfy its prerequisites. (See Gal. 3:10-12). Christ redeemed us from that curse by taking the curse of death upon himself. In this way he redeemed us from the curse.

The death of Christ was a vicarious work. It was substitutionary. He accomplished something for us which we couldn't do for ourselves.

Jesus said that he came to give his life a ransom for (anti, instead of) many (Matt. 20:28; Mark 10:45). The relational word utilized here indicates substitution. The relational words typically utilized don't inside themselves mean substitution (peri and huper). It is said that he dies for, or on behalf of, miscreants (sinners).

However, this does not prohibit the possibility of substitution. A thing might be done for, or on behalf of, one by being in his place or stead. So when it is said that Christ dies for our transgressions (sins) (I Cor.15:3), or on behalf of us (Rom. 5:8), this might be done in the method for substitution (huper, peri would have about a same significance). In any case, when it is said that he gave his life a ransom in the stead or place of (anti), many, it can hardly be anything besides substitution.

Christ, at that point, in his redeeming work was propitiatory. In exemplary Greek, to propitiate intends to render favorable. Christ did not render favorable, but rather he so dealt with human sin as to make it feasible for God to demonstrate his favor in salvation. Paul says that God set him forth as propitiatory in his blood (Rom. 3:25).

John says that he is the propitiation, for our transgressions (sins), as well as for the sins of the whole world (I John 2:2). The book of Hebrews says that as a faithful high priest he makes propitiation for the transgressions (sins) of the people (Heb. 2:17). The Christian thought isn't that God must be satisfied before he will have mercy or love to the sinner, however it is somewhat that God's holy character responds against wrongdoing (sin) and that transgression (sin) intervenes a hindrance (a barrier) between God and the heathen (sinner) so God can't be steady with his own moral character and save the miscreant (sinner) until the barrier is removed.

God isn't vindictive, but he has respect to his own moral consistency. The propitiatory work of Christ is the revelation and articulation of God's affection (love).

It is far fetched, in any case, if Paul intends to state that Christ in his death was propitiatory as in the sense that God was pleased with his death separated from its result in saving man. This typical elucidation has put the accentuation on the blood as propitiatory. However, Paul says that God put forth Christ as propitiatory, through faith, in his blood.

John does not say that Christ's death was a propitiation. He says rather that Christ was such a propitiation. He didn't die to buy God's favor. He came rather as the revelation of God's love.

Nor should Paul's expression, through faith, be ignored, as it for the most part may be, as though it were incidental, very nearly an idea in retrospect.

Christ in his blood opened up the way for man to come to God through faith, and the result, that is, man's coming to God, was pleasing to God. God was propitiated as in the sense when the miscreant (sinner) exercises faith, God can present mercy instead of wrath.

A Difficulty Considered

What the objector needs to remember:

A. THERE ARE NO guiltless individuals, none righteous, all men are sinners, all men are liable of wrongdoing (sin), the whole world order, rest under the curse of sin. In our race, there are just generally innocent men, none who are totally so. This curse speaks to the judgment of God.

God's judgment is on the whole human order of life. One who recognizes himself with man for his redemption must share the curse. This curse on man and his reality speaks to the reaction of God's holy character on human sin. This causes us to comprehend what is implied by the propitiatory character of Christ's death.

Man's moral judgment endorses the idea that the guilty ought to suffer. Man's moral judgment would likewise endorse the idea that the individuals who would deliver the blameworthy (guilty) from the curse of transgression (sin) should partake in the suffering of the guilty.

b. It is a law of life that men should suffer over the wrongs (sins) of others. Regardless of what we may state about the justice or injustice of it, this is a reality. What's more, it is hard to perceive how it could be generally otherwise in a social world. A game plan by which one would suffer the correct deserts of his wrongdoings (sins) and no one else suffer over them would scarcely be a social world by any means.

What's more, the facts demonstrate that the blameless, the innocent suffer over the guilty. Occurrences are too various to even consider needing notice. This is one limited from wickedness by the cognizance that others will suffer on the instance that they sin. Additionally, the facts demonstrate that quite a bit of our moral improvement originates from suffering on behalf of others. It is a law of the Christian life that one should be willing to follow the Savior's example in doing this.

c. The most elevated articulation of love is found in this Christian law of ability to suffer in the interest of others. This was the crowning glory of the life of Christ and is what denotes a man as a devotee (follower) of Christ. If any man hath not the Spirit of Christ, he is none of his (Rom. 8:9).

It is love that moved Christ to give himself for us. If it is held that one couldn't bear the wrongdoings (sin) of another, that would be identical to stating that love in that respect was limited. In other words, in the very domain where one most needs assistance, in the moral and spiritual, the domain of our transgressions (sins) and disappointments (failures), love is feeble to render service.

d. Also, this complaint depends on a bogus supposition (false assumption). The complaint says that it would be unjustifiable for God to lay the wrongdoings (sins) of one man on another man. Be that as it may, there are two things to be said in reply to this. One is that God did not take our transgressions (sins) and lay them on a reluctant injured individual (an unwilling victim). Christ took our transgressions (sins) on himself. As a matter of love, he intentionally expected our commitment. He laid down his life of himself (John 10:18).

Once more, the complaint accept that Christ is only a single human individual among other human people. Maybe the dissenter would be right in saying that one human individual couldn't bear the transgressions (sins) of endless other human people.

The relation of Christ to any man or to the race all in all is altogether unique in relation to the relation of one who is just a human individual to his kindred men or to his race. The race exists in Christ. It was in and through him that the race was created and is preserved (John 1:3; Col. 1:165,17). He is, in this way, the creator of the whole moral order that has been damaged by man's wrongdoing (sins).

The death of Christ, for our transgressions (sins) does not imply that God laid the weight of our wrongdoings (sins) on a vulnerable human individual, but rather that in the individual of Christ. God himself got under the weight (burdens) of our transgressions (sins) to save us. The work of Christ is the work of God.

Our faith in Jesus throws light on his redemptive work. We confide in him as Savior from wrongdoing (sin). We come to him confessing ourselves morally and spiritually bankrupt. We perceive that we have no standing of our own before a heavenly, holy God. For such standing we should trust ourselves into his hands.

We recognize ourselves subordinate (we are dependent on God) upon him in the most critical all things considered, the moral and spiritual; and in the most central all things considered, our relation with God.

We confess ourselves precluded to deal with God as holy in our own name; our wrongdoings (sins) have excluded us. Christ is qualified for all requirements to deal with God for us.

What's more, the New Testament clarifies that what qualifies him to deal with God for our benefit or on our behalf is his dying for us. This sets his death as the ground of our acceptance with God over against our wrongdoings (sins) as the ground of our rejection. Our transgressions (sins) constitutes the premise of our moral standing before God.

The Cross And The Love Of God

ONE THING EMERGES OBVIOUSLY in the New Testament, and should never be clouded; to be specific, that Christ's death came out of, and communicates, God's love for us. Any view that denies this is against Christianity (anti-Christian), and any view that clouds this does not have that quite a bit of being completely Christian and it is a marvel that any individual who denies this is a Christian by any means.

Love The Motive Of Redemption

THE THOUGHT PROCESS (MOTIVE) of redemption is the love for God. "God so loved the world, that he gave his only begotten Son" (John 3:16). "God commendeth his love toward us, in that, while we were yet sinners, Christ died for us" (Rom. 5:8). Christ did not die to win for men the affection of God, but as an expression of that adoration (love).

It is a crime on the New Testament perspective of this precept to speak to it as implying that God was the embodiment of justice and Christ the embodiment of love and that Christ died to win for man the love of God.

The love of Christ for heathens (sinners) was the love of God. The death of Christ was the love of God in real life (God's love in action), looking to redeem men from transgression (sin); it was love heading off to the furthest reaches of anguish and distress to redeem the lost from the ruin of their own sin.

The cross of Christ is the promise of God's love for a sinful and ruin race. So the cross speaks to a demonstration of grace. It represents God's gracious love going out to redeem man as sinful and contemptible.

This is one reason that we should insist that the death of Christ was in excess of a martyr's death. His death speaks to something more significant than the deed of a man for us. Athanasius and the individuals who remained with him in early Christian history for the idea that the Son was of the same substance with the Father contended that no one but God could reveal God and no one but God could save man.

The cross, in this way, in Christian history has dependably symbolized something God did for man and not what man did. One who was only a man couldn't accomplish something that would reveal the affection (love) for God. This is likewise contradictory to the idea that it was only the human nature of Christ that suffered, not his perfect, divine nature. All things considered, the cross represents what mankind did, not what God did for man.

The Moral Influence Theory

Up until now, the individuals who have supported the moral influence theory would concur. This theory denies that Christ's death was substitutionary. There was nothing of the nature of penalty in his sufferings. There is nothing in the way for rage in God to be satisfied before God can forgive sin.

Christ died just as a disclosure of love for the delinquent (sinner). The main trouble in the method for the sinner's salvation is on the heathen's (sinner's) part, not on God's. If the miscreant (sinner) will only repent, God stands prepared to forgive. The purpose behind the death of Christ is to show the affection for God and in this way lead the delinquent (sinner) to repent.

It shares much for all intents and purpose with the example theory. Alongside that view, it objects to the possibility that one individual should die in the spot of another. One may suffer thoughtfully with and over another. Particularly does it demand this is true with reference to the penalty of transgression (sin). There is a strong propensity among those holding this view to make love the controlling attribute in God, to the disregard or disavowal of anything like retributive righteousness. Suffering is viewed as basically, if not solely, therapeutic, remedial.

One complaint or objection to this theory is that it inclines toward a brain science of religion (psychology of religion) that diminishes the guilt of wrongdoing (sin) to a guilt awareness that has no goal ground. It says that the main trouble in the method for the delinquent's salvation is in the heathen (sinner), not in God. That adds up to stating that man's guilt awareness is a fantasy. His feeling of sick desert is grim.

This sort of religious experience that we find in Bunyan, Luther, Carey, or Paul is strange and meddles with the advancement of the correct kind of Christian character.

What men need isn't salvation from guilt and condemnation, but salvation from their consciousness of guilt and condemnation.

Be that as it may, if man's religious consciousness is deceptive in regard to guilt and condemnation, for what reason may it not be additionally with reference to God's love and mercy? For what reason should our religious consciousness be dependable with respect to one and not concerning the other? The awareness or consciousness of guilt and condemnation has been as altogether implanted in the experience of Christians as the cognizance of the love for God.

Indeed, in experience the two go together. This is the teaching of Jesus in Luke 7:40 ff. At any rate it is engaged with what Jesus says. He demonstrate that one who is most conscious of sins forgiven will love most. He is addressing the Pharisees who had no feeling of need of absolution (forgiveness). He says in substance: "You don't love since you have not had any sense of sins pardoned."

It is just as we have a consciousness of transgression (sin) and blame (guilt) that we have such a cognizance of the grace of God in saving from wrongdoing (sin) as to call out our adoration to God. The love for God isn't amplified at that point, however limited, by limiting the blame (guilt) and condemnation of wrongdoing (sin). This has its bearing on practical Christian activity.

The men that have had a profound feeling of blame (guilt), trailed by a cognizance of salvation through the grace of God, have been the incredible evangelists, preachers, and manufacturers in the kingdom of God. They have been the men who have started new periods in the headway of Christianity on the planet.

This consciousness of condemnation is excessively essentially related with the cognizance of affection for God to clarify the previous as subjective and illusory while holding that the last is consistent with the real world. It is simpler to clarify the experience of the individuals who don't have an unmistakable consciousness of guilt as because of an absence of spiritual discernment on their part than to clarify the cognizance of guilt with respect to those who do have it as being only subjective and illusory.

We hold that the feeling of blame (guilt) is so essential a factor in the Christian cognizance that to decrease that feeling of blame (guilt) to hallucination intends to refute the Christian consciousness inside and out and arrive us in religious skepticism.

Another complaint to the ethical impact hypothesis of the expiation is that it outfits no reasonable association between the demise of Christ and the conclusion to be cultivated by it. The vicarious or substitutionary see furnishes a reasonable clarification of the association between the two.

The conclusion to be cultivated by the substitutionary see is our redemption from the judgment that happens upon us on account of our transgressions. Christ achieves that end by going up against himself the revile because of our wrongdoing. He passed on in our place. As indicated by the moral influence theory, the conclusion to be cultivated is such a disclosure of the affection for God as will divert delinquents (sinners) from their transgressions.

In any case, the inquiry emerges: How is the passing of Christ an indication of the adoration for God? What is the association between his death and our transgression that makes his dying an appearance of God's affection to us? The vicarious view answers this inquiry by saying that Christ's death was bearing the name of our curse; it was such an indication of the anger of God against wrongdoing (sin) as to make it conceivable that God could be righteous but then legitimize the penitent sinner.

The moral influence theory has no response to the inquiry. At the end of the day, this theory can demonstrate nothing in the moral connections to require the death of Christ as the ground of our salvation. The representations of Dr. Denny's

Death of Jesus and of Dr. Mullins' The Christian Religion are in point. If a father should dive himself into the water and suffocate himself, or push his hand into the flame and consume it off, this would not be a sign of affection to the father's kid except if the father brought about the misfortune to save the youngster from a risk of suffocating in the one case or consuming in the other.

It would prefer to be a sign of imprudence. So except if the heathen (sinner) rests under a condemnation that jeopardizes his spiritual welfare, how is the death of Christ a sign of the adoration for God to the miscreant (sinner)?

This view, in any case, has the benefit of underscoring one of the fundamental things in the New Testament: to be specific, that Christ died on account of God's love for men lost in transgression (sin).

We should always remember, nonetheless, that the affection of God show in the cross of Christ is heavenly love. It is love that is interminably restricted to sin, effectively contradicted to sin. In that capacity it is righteous. Righteousness and love, at that point, are not contradictory or restricted to one another. Both signify the moral perfection or holiness of God.

Love is never minor friendliness nor moral lack of concern; moral righteousness is its core. What's more, righteousness dependably has love at its inside. Regardless of whether we think about the moral nature of God as love or righteousness, it is against transgression (sin). It looks to beat sin, and the cross is the strategy used to overcome sin.

The Cross As Victory Over Sin

The Ransom Theory

1. ONE OF THE most punctual perspectives with reference to the saving work of Christ was known as the ransom theory. It was never detailed in any unequivocal way and could scarcely be talked about as an unmistakable theory. It won pretty much for the most part to something like a thousand years.

It had related with it such remarkable names in Christian history as Origen and Augustine. Since a significant number of the names of the early church fathers were related with the view, it is once in a while talked about as the "patristic" see. It was the closest thing to a distinct theory of the atonement in Christian history until Anselm's day.

The view had for a scriptural foundation or establishment such passages as the saying of Jesus that the Son of man came to give his life a ransom for many (Mark 10:45) and various different passages in which his work is talked about as a redeeming or ransoming from transgression (sin) and its power. When the inquiry emerged about whom the ransom was paid, a large number of the early fathers said that it was paid to the devil.

All general outline, with varieties, the view was that the devil in the Fall procured a right over humankind; God redeemed man from his oppressed (enslaved condition) condition by delivering Christ in death to the fallen angel (the devil), as per terms of an agreement. In any case, in the resurrection Christ conquered the devil and he was left pillaged (despoiled) of both Christ and humankind.

Once in a while an element of misdirection (deceit) and slyness (trickery) was brought into the theory, in that the devil was offered Christ in death in return for the race. The devil was uninformed of Christ's holiness, or his divinity. Christ, be that as it may, being divine conquered, overcame the devil and thus robbed him denied him of his victim.

Sin As Opposition To God

2. UNREFINED AS THIS view seemed to be, it really speaks to sin and salvation as a conflict between God and the devil. It is a conflict that is more than human and more than person. It is a conflict between a kingdom of light and one of obscurity (darkness) between God at the head of the powers of righteousness and Satan at the head of the powers of evil.

Some ongoing authors have shown that a genuine perspective of Christ's saving work would need to pursue this line instead of the lines of the "moral" or "penal" views. As I comprehend them, they intend to state that we should think about Christ's saving work just like being the defeating of spiritual opposition to God and the death of Christ as the means by which this was accomplished.

I can't help suspecting this is a genuine understanding. From the earliest starting point of mankind's history sin has been resistance (opposition) to God. Additionally, it has been in excess of a human clash. Man fell, under allurement from a superhuman source. We wrestle not with flesh and blood alone. Sin is detestable, diabolical in its nature.

Also, sin develops over against righteousness. The higher the manifestation of righteousness nature the more unpretentious and extreme does the opposition progress toward becoming. Paul discusses "the passions of sins which were through the law" (Rom. 7:5). The law turns into an event for the development of transgression.

A large portion of whatever is left of the chapter is a piece of what the missionary means by that statement. He demonstrates that before we come into ownership of good light sin is a sleeping guideline in us. When we come to have moral light (the law) and realize what is correct, we don't play out the right. Rather than that, transgression (sin) stirs to lively activity and man is subjugated by its power. No one but Christ can deliver from its power.

Jesus shows that the condemnation of the people to whom he ministered would be more prominent than that of the general population of Sodom and Gomorrah or of Tyre and Sidon.

This was genuine on the grounds that the general population of Chorazin, Capernaum, and Bethsaida had more prominent light and privilege, and henceforth more noteworthy guilt.

In John's Gospel Jesus says: "If I had not come and spoken unto them, they had not had sin"; and, "If I had not done among them the works which none other did, they had not had sin" (John 15:22, 24).

Presently, he says, they have no cloak or excuse for their transgression (sin). What made their wrongdoing (sin) so horrible was that they had seen both him and the Father (v. 24).

His presence in their midst as the light of the world implied that they should acknowledge that light and turn to God or else turn permanently to sin and death. It is certainly along this line we are to comprehend the warning in Matthew 12:31. Jesus was in their midst doing the work of God under the power of God's Spirit. They were profanely (blasphemously) saying that his works were works of the devil.

They couldn't deny his strong works, but they were stating that they were devilish in character. Anyone who might along these lines intentionally call white dark was in risk of putting out his very own spiritual eyes thus perverting his very own moral nature that it would be a moral inconceivability (impossibility) for God to save him. He would perpetually fix his very own character in sin.

So we see that the character of sin is such and the character of God's holiness or righteousness is with the end goal that there is an unavoidable clash or conflict between the two. This conflict has been going on since the start of mankind's history and will go on to its end. The Fourth Gospel (John) alludes to this conflict when it says: "The light shineth in the darkness, and the darkness did not secure (or better maybe, survive, or overcome) it" (John 1:5). This conflict is spoken to in John's Gospel as an unending battle among light and darkness.

This view, obviously, would be conflicting with a flat out or absolute monism. It depends on the suspicion that man has moral freedom and responsibility and that wrongdoing (sin) is genuine, real opposition or restriction to God. It is monotheistic in its interpretation of the world but not monistic. Sin is more than shortcoming, weakness or immaturity; it is deliberate disobedience to the will of God.

The Conflict In The Life of Jesus

3. THE LIFE OF Jesus was one of contention with evil completely through. Amid his early stages the powers of evil were trying to decimate him, so his folks needed to escape with him to Egypt. From his passageway into his public ministry, he was plagued with trial and temptation, but was constantly victorious.

So far as we are given light on his allurements and battles, they centered in his mission and how he should fulfill that mission. His messianic mission was not a part of his life it was all of his life. He lived for the one thing of fulfilling his mission. His meat was to do his Father's will and complete the work that God had given him to do.

The central question in his life was not whether he should do the work assigned him, but how he should do it. What strategy and means would it be a good idea for him to use to take every necessary step assigned to him? By what method would it be a good idea for him to continue to introduce God's kingdom on earth? Would it be a good idea for him to speak to dynamite techniques, perform supernatural occurrences

Dr. John Thomas Wylie

that would flabbergast the large number and win a mainstream following?

Would it be advisable for him to engage military or physical power and repress his foes with compelling force? Such inquiries as these shaped the focal point of his battle in the wild and in the extraordinary emergencies of his life, even up to Gethsemane.

He had come to set up the righteous reign of God among men. The inquiry was what the nature of the reign should be and how it should be established. Evil must be ousted; however, how should that be possible? The strategies used to set up the reign of God must conform to the nature of the kingdom to be established. A spiritual reign couldn't be built up by military strategies.

God can reign in the lives of men just by their free consent and by their dynamic cooperation. Thus the methods utilized must be, for example, such would verify that outcome. This wasn't possible by military or political power. God can utilize military power to devastate military power, but he can't utilize military or political power to set up a spiritual kingdom. The history of Christianity is an exhibition of the uselessness of the utilization of carnal means and strategies for advancing spiritual ends.

Jesus saw that adoration was the only power that would be viable in building up a kingdom of love. He made love, in this way, the focal standard in religion. Be that as it may, Jesus saw something else. He saw that love in the sort of world in which he lived would be executed. He cautioned the disciples that following him would mean persecution.

He knew how the Old Testament prophets had been dealt with, and he comprehended what carrying on with a real existence of love would do to him and what it would mean to the individuals who followed him. There is a critical articulation about Cain in I John 3:11,12. It says that Cain slew his brother for the reason that his very own works were malicious (evil) while his brother's were good. The nature of sin is with the end goal that it battles the good. It would not be malevolent (evil) if it didn't.

So Jesus was executed as a result of his integrity, his goodness. The insidious powers of his day were undoubtedly bound to kill him. They couldn't live with him. What else would they be able to do? They should slaughter him or stop to be detestable. Then again, if Jesus had stopped utilizing the technique for love and had embraced the strategy for common power, that would have ceased to be righteous and would have lost the power of righteousness, the power of love.

When the devil attempted to motivate Jesus to compromise by worshiping him, Jesus saw this was not the best approach to win but rather to lose. By compromising with evil Jesus would have lost everything. His mission would have fizzled and evil would have triumphed.

John discloses to us that God is love (I John 4:8, 16). This makes love the pith of God's being. the penal view will in general make retributive justice the key or controlling attribute of God. The New Testament makes nothing more basic than love in God. Since God is love, to state that love and evil are in conflict with one another is to state that God and evil are in conflict.

This was the assurance that, in the account of Jesus, love should triumph over evil. At the point when Jesus was executed as a malefactor, killed between two culprits (criminals), it appeared that evil was certainly lastly triumphant over righteousness and truth. He was harassed, hounded by jealousy, desire, envy, and perniciousness, charged by false witnesses and put to death as a criminal.

However, it is to be noticed that the Jewish Sanhedrin sentenced him to death on the ground of his own admission that he was the Messiah, the Son of God. The mystery is by all accounts that in affectation, superficially, he was executed as an evildoer and a criminal, but as a general rule he was condemned as the Messiah of God, the Savior of the world. It was sin that killed him, and he was executed as God's Messiah.

The Cross As The Climax Of This Conflict

4. THIS CONFLICT ALONG these lines went to its peak in the cross of Christ. Here light and darkness, holiness and sin, God and the devil came into lethal battle. One side or the other should forever be conquered. Holiness and truth here always vanquished sin and shrewdness (evil). God could oppose sin in one of two ways. One is by punishing the heathen (sinner); the other by redeeming him.

The former technique gives a fractional but obvious disclosure of God. It uncovers the component of retributive justice in God. The second technique gives a last disclosure of God's character as grace that saves. We don't come to the Christian origination of God until we realize God as grace, but we will never know him in any character that is higher than grace.

Such is a moral impossibility. This gives finality in the disclosure of God's character as grace.

The strategy for redemption invalidates sin; punishment only smothers (suppresses it) it. A criminal might be limited by justice; grace transforms him into a holy person.

In this view the cross was unavoidable if the incarnation is granted (Mullins, 1959). If Christ is God come as an immaculate (sinless) man into a fallen race, the cross was unavoidable. All things considered, the immaculate Christ is certain to carry on with an actual existence of service to men and they are certain to kill him. Each acts his part.

This view not just aligns the incarnation with the cross. It additionally makes redemption the work of God right through. It has been standard among backers of the penal view, from the times of Anselm on, to see the amends as man's work, not God's, as in it was held that it was the human nature of Christ that endured, not the divine.

The facts confirm that Anselm and his adherents held that Christ was divine, but they held that he suffered only in his human nature. His divine nature, it is stated, offered dignity to his person and thus gave expanded esteem (interminable or for all intents and purposes so) to his sufferings.

These sufferings must be of infinite indignity to offset the limitless suffered by the honor (or justice) of God. In any case, while the divine nature of Christ gave infinite value to his person and thus to his sufferings, it was held that the divine nature did not suffer, since God was impassible. He couldn't suffer.

The idea that Christ acted by his two natures, it is possible that one administering his activity as per the circumstance autonomously of the other while the other offered an incentive to what he did, sums to preventing the truth from claiming the incarnation.

We are not here endeavoring to explain the secret of the incarnation, but we are arguing on the assumption of its reality. But if the natures lay one next to the other in his person and he could act as accordingly by either nature autonomously of the other, then God did not progress toward becoming man, he only took nature as a sort of coat which was only an article of clothing he wore, not a part of him. All things considered God drew close to man; he didn't progress toward becoming man. This would not be a genuine incarnation.

Furthermore, if there was no divine misery, there was no divine sacrifice for sins, and the redeeming death of Christ was a human demonstration, not a divine accomplishment. This isn't the New Testament view. The New Testament view is that in Christ God moved toward became man and that his work in saving us - all his work in saving us - is God's work. God himself got under the burden of our wrongdoings (sins). He accomplished our recovery.

The revelation of God as love contradicts the idea that God can't suffer. A God who loves must suffer when his world is attacked or invaded by sin and men are destroyed by it. To state that God does not suffer is to say that he couldn't care less.

Victory Manifest In The Resurrection

WHEN JESUS DIED ON the cross it gave the seemed that wrongdoing (sin) and death had prevailed. However, not so actually. He triumphed over transgression (sin) and death. He conquered death because he conquered sin. Peter was correct when he said that he couldn't be holden of death (Acts 2:24). He seemed by all accounts to be conquered by sin, however, he had conquered sin and along these lines rose victorious over death.

In this way the conflict among Christ and sin that finished in death issued in resurrection. Sin and death go together. They are parts of one whole. Death isn't something that God subjectively incurs on the miscreant (sinner). Dr. Mullins (1959) discusses the sin death guideline. This is in accordance with the New Testament. Paul intently interfaces sin and death in the entirety of his dialogs.

This turns out unmistakably in such passages as Romans chapters 5-8. "The wages of sin is death" (6:23). The individuals who live as per the flesh are going to die (8:13).

The legitimized man isn't under judgment, in light of the fact that the law of the Spirit of life (the control of the Spirit that produces life) has liberated him from the law (control) of wrongdoing (sin) and death. Sin and death are Siamese twins. They are inseparable.

Christ conquered sin and death because on the grounds that he was the incarnation of God. This conflict was not among man and sin. Sin had won that challenge since the beginning. However at this point God, in the person of Christ, participated in the challenge for man, and won in the conflict.

The resurrection was the finished annihilation of sin, death, and the devil. Jesus did die as an unfortunate casualty; he died as a victor. His triumph was show in the resurrection. He said that no man took his life from him. He laid it down of himself, and of himself he took it once more (John 10:18). The penal theory regards Jesus as an unfortunate casualty, however he died as a conqueror.

In dying he conquered death and Hades. This resurrection of Jesus is the watershed of New Testament Christianity. It denotes the mainland separate. To change the figure a bit, it denotes the point where we go up onto a higher plane, however we don't descend again.

The resurrection of Jesus was the height of his whole personality to a higher plane of being. It gives us a widespread, spiritual Christ rather than a nearby, constrained Christ. Numerous individuals think back with yearning to the Christ of the Lake or the Galilean slopes. It was obviously magnificent for the disciples to have Christ present with them in the flesh.

However, we today have something more superb, more wonderful than that. We have a Christ who in his resurrection was raised over the constraints of existence (limits of time and space).

Let us view some specific New Testament passages on this matter: One is an announcement from Matthew in which Jesus is spoken to as saying, "All authority hath been given unto me in paradise and on earth" (Matt. 28:18). Subsequent to providing for his disciples the great commission on this premise (see the "therefore" of verse 19) he says once more, "And lo, I am with you always, even unto the end of the world (the apocalypse)" (Matt. 28:20).

This is a post-restoration explanation of Jesus. Notice the all inclusive range of the authority here claimed as given him. It is authority that came to be his. Clearly it is authority given to him in the resurrection.

It speaks to his triumph over sin and death. Then he promises his spiritual omnipresence with his people as they carry out his command.

In a pre-resurrection proclamation he promises to be in their midst at whatever point a few are assembled in his name (Matt. 18:20). Obviously Jesus is anticipating his post-resurrection state and his relation to his disciples in this promise.

Another critical proclamation is found in Acts 2:36. Peter says, "Let all the house of Israel therefore know assuredly that God hath made him both Lord and Christ, this Jesus whom ye crucified." Peter is here disclosing to his listeners the centrality of what has recently occurred upon the day of Pentecost.

He clarifies that the Holy Spirit has been spilled out by the risen and exalted Christ. In fulfillment of Psalm 110:1, God has raised Jesus from the dead and exalted him to a position of authority and power at his right hand. Jesus who has exalted, having received from the Father the promised Holy Spirit, has poured forth this which they currently see and hear.

Then he says that the noteworthiness of the whole thing, so far as Jesus is concerned, is that God has made this Jesus whom they have crucified both Lord and Christ. God did this in the resurrection and ascension. This is evidenced by the coming of the Holy Spirit.

What does it mean when he says that God has made Jesus both Lord and Christ? The name Jesus means the person whom they have known as living in their midst and whom they have killed (crucified).

Now Peter announces to them the startling reality that God has turned around their judgment of condemnation upon Jesus and lifted up him to a position of authority and power that rightly belongs to him as Lord and Christ. The position he involved before in their midst was not the position that was legitimately his. He was present as one limited or restricted in power, as one described by humility, even by weakness as appeared in his being put to a dishonorable death. This position is his no more.

God has exalted him. God has dressed him with universal authority and power. This power is spiritual in its nature as shown by the overflowing of the Holy Spirit. It is moral, not physical or

Dr. John Thomas Wylie

military, in character. That is ensured in the way that it is the same Jesus whom they had known and who had died instead of allowing his disciples to utilize force in protecting him or as opposed to call upon heavenly spiritual power as represented in the angels to defend him.

The book of Acts is composed to set forward the activity of this exalted Christ. Luke's first treatise was about what Jesus began to do and teach (Acts 1:1). The program of the risen Christ is set forth in Acts 1:8. Whatever rest of the book is to demonstrate how the evangelistic and missionary activity of the early disciples was the carrying out of this program as the ascended Christ worked by his Spirit through his people.

From Pentecost on in the New Testament, the presence and activity of the Spirit are constantly viewed as the spiritual presence and activity of the glorified Jesus. By his Spirit he is present with his people and works in and through them to set up his kingdom on earth.

Does not Paul in Rom. 1:4 mean the same thing as Peter in Acts 2:36? Not simply, as the interpretations (translations) would show, that Jesus by resurrection was declared or demonstrated to be the Son of God, but rather that God in the resurrection instated Jesus in a position of power that was as per his higher spiritual nature (as indicated by the spirit of holiness). He has recently demonstrated that on the human side (as indicated by the flesh) he was conceived of the seed of David. In any case, the position that he held while living among men on earth did not relate to his higher nature, the spirit of holiness.

But when God raised him from the dead he brought him into a position of power that corresponded to his higher nature. Amid his earthly life his higher nature was restricted, confined, one may state, in a state or condition of humiliation into which he voluntarily came for man's redemption.

The resurrection was his release. It was his liberation day. The limits were removed. The everlasting doors were lifted up and the King of Glory marched to his throne. This interpretation is supported by the specific situation and fits in commendably with the origination put forward by Paul in different places, and by the Whole New Testament concerning the glorified Christ.

Basically a similar view is associated with what Paul says in I Corinthians 15:20-28. Christ is the first fruits from the dead. Having risen from the dead, he presently reigns at the right hand of God. There he will remain until he has abolished all rule and authority and power. That is, each opponent, rival, or opposing force known to mankind will be subdued.

The climax of this conquering reign will come when Christ comes back again to raise the bodies of his people from the dead. Everything will at that point have been subdued by Christ aside from God alone who has oppressed all things unto Christ.

Maybe the most exceptional passage in the New Testament on this inquiry is Philippians 2:9-11. Here Paul says that God highly exalted Christ, and gave unto him the name which is over every name. He has supreme place in the universe of God. Each knee is to bow to him, of things in paradise, on earth, and under the earth. Each tongue will confess that he is Lord to the glory of God the Father.

This absolute lordship comes to Christ as a moral reward for his deliberate humiliation and death. Since he emptied himself, God exalted him. This thought we endeavored to express by saying that Christ won his supreme victory in submission to death.

In the book of Revelation John records his vision of the glorified Christ in the first chapter (vv. 10-20). He shows up in his glory and power. His feet that had been penetrated are currently feet of shined metal. The strength of the sun is in his face. He holds the messengers of the places of worship in his hand and walks in majesty among the churches.

A sharp two-edged sword proceeds out of his mouth. The Son of God goes forward to war. The book of Revelation gives us a perspective of the war that he conducts against darkness and sin. That war never stops until sin is vanished and righteousness and truth rule in God's world.

Numerous other passages bearing regarding this matter could be given from the New Testament, but it is pointless to cite them. The whole New Testament from the Gospels on is composed from the perspective of the risen, ruling Christ. He is no longer restricted, (limited) as he was amid the times of his flesh. He is presently, now the conquering Christ. He is himself the supreme example of the spiritual law that one wins life through death.

The Gospel of John speaks about his death as his being lifted up over the confinements that he encountered in the flesh. He was glorified in death. Through death he came to the glory and power that were rightly his as the Son of God.

When he conquered sin and death on the cross and manifested his victory in the resurrection, he brought life and immorality status for all who believe in him. He became the wellspring of eternal life to all who were joined to him by faith. He became the source and the head of a new humanity that is being created in the spiritual image of God. He is himself the active agent in the making of such a humanity.

We bring to mind again that articulation happening a few times in the New Testament that Christ sat down at the right hand of God.

He sat down as a victor. He had achieved the undertaking of making a complete Once and for all offering for sin.

He takes a seat to reign. God has placed him on the throne of David to rule eternally, forever(Acts 2:29 ff.). Every one of his adversaries have not yet been put underneath his feet, however they will be sometime in the future (I Cor. 15:24 ff.; Heb. 2:5 ff.).

The Risen Christ And The Spirit

THE CROSS AND RESTORATION of Jesus comprise the ground of triumph over wickedness on an infinite scale. However the triumph, while final on a basic level, must be broadened. They didn't consummate the kingdom; they established it. The cross is the ground and establishment of each victory that God's people will ever prevail over evil until the completed and eternal kingdom of God will come.

As victor over sin and death, Christ sends the Spirit on his people. He shed forth the Spirit upon the day of Pentecost (Acts 2:33). He is now the living, super-historical Christ. All things considered he sheds forward his Spirit on his people. And the work of the Spirit is to make him Savior and Lord in the lives of men. The Spirit is the Spirit of Christ (Rom. 8:9).

The coming of the Spirit is the coming of Christ. The Spirit's presence is presence of Christ. Pentecost was the extension in the lives of men to the redemptive power of the death and resurrection of Jesus.

The living Christ acts upon human life from above. He acts on mankind's history in a perpendicular way, not just in a horizontal way. He pours fresh accessions of spiritual power into human life and history. He renews history. That is the only hope of the world.

With reference to this, notice two books in the New Testament. One is the book of Acts. This book isn't recounting the demonstrations of the witnesses. Just two of the missionaries have much noticeable quality in the book. One of them was Saul of Tarsus, whom the living Christ vanquished and appointed as a missionary preacher to the Gentiles.

His missionary exercises pose a potential threat in the last half. In the prior half Peter is the fundamental human on-screen character. John gets some notice, however very little. whatever is left of the missionaries are barely referenced. If Christianity relied upon apostolic succession, the writer of this book scarcely had the right perspective.

Luke tells Theophilus (1:1) that in his previous treatise (the Gospel) he has recorded what Jesus started to do and instruct. The genuine subject of the book, at that point is the demonstrations or deeds of the living Christ. He is the focal performing artist. He works through his people, by the Spirit, for the coming of his kingdom.

The book of Revelation depicts a similar thought. The living Christ shows up in the first chapter with the strength of the sun sparkling from his face and a sharp two-edged sword proceeding out of his mouth. He is a militant Christ. The Son of God goes forth to war, and he keeps on making war on sin and darkness until these are driven out of the world and the perfected kingdom of God has come.

We have a few signs in this book regarding how he is to function. He moves amidst the candles, which are the holy places (churches). He holds the seven stars in his right hand. These are maybe a symbol for the places of worship or their pastors. These two images would appear to demonstrate that the living Christ identifies himself with his people and that they are to be his agents in his work.

The sharp, two-edged sword speaks to the gospel, or the expression of God, which he is to utilize. We find likewise later that this Christ is envisioned as the Lion of the tribe of Judah. Here is his power. Be that as it may, his supremacy is spiritual in character, for as we see the Lion of the tribe of Judah he becomes the Lamb slain. His power is the power of sacrificial love. It is by the blood of the Lamb and the word of their testimony that his followers conquer the devil (12:11).

Chapter
FIVE

The Cross And The Christian Life

The Christian As Sharing The Cross

1. IF THE CROSS of Christ is central in our salvation, we should find in the New Testament that the Christian life is translated regarding the cross; and that is exactly what we find. Jesus more than once said to his disciples that they should deny all, take up the cross, and follow him (Mark 8:34 ff.; Luke 14:25 ff.; et al.).

In John's Gospel he said that unless if a grain of wheat "fall into the ground and die, it abideth alone; but if it die, it bringeth forward much fruit" (John 12:24). Paul talks about the Christian as one who has died to sin, been buried with Christ and ascended to newness of life (Rom. 6:1 ff.).

He says of himself that he has been crucified; yet he lives, in that Christ lives in him by faith (Gal. 2:20). Peter admonishes Christians to suffer, after the example of Christ, not as evildoers, but as the those who are righteous (I Pet. 2:20 ff.; 4:12 ff.). We believe that these passages, with others that may be taken from the New Testament, justify the statement that one can't be a Christian except the spirit of the cross is found in his life.

These passages clarify that the cross is something that the Christian is to share. Zealous Christianity has stressed that Christians reincarnate Christ. Christ was the manifestation of God, and through Christ God is being resurrected in his people in the world.

God means for making himself known on the planet today is through those in whom the Spirit of God abides. They speak to him, not in any remotely official way, however in that they are the living exemplification of his Spirit. This is one of the lines on which ecclesiology partitions. Some hold that the church represents Christ since he committed to it his authority with the goal that what the church does it dos by the authority of Christ.

Normally there is related with this sort of ecclesiology the possibility of biblical progression in some structure. The Roman Catholic Church is a decent delegate of this kind of ecclesiology. there is another sort that holds that the church is the portrayal of Christ, since it epitomizes his Spirit, and that the movement of the church represents Christ and his power just as the church is really the spiritual body of Christ, typifying and communicating his will in the world; but

Dr. John Thomas Wylie

that the church represents the authority of Christ to the extent that it embodies and expresses his Spirit.

While evangelical Christianity has held that the church as the body of Christ, was in this manner an expansion of the incarnation, it has been moderate (slow) to apply a same rule to the cross of Christ. There appeared to be a dread that, if this guideline were connected to the cross, it would wreck the uniqueness of Christ's saving work can be lost.

That has been done on account of the incarnation by the individuals who substituted for the evangelical teaching of the incarnation the idea of an incarnation of God in humankind all in all, denying that Christ was the incarnation of God in any exceptional or select sense.

Christ was looked on as the Son of God only as all other men were the sons of God. All men were viewed as divine. The outcome was that, by worshiping everything and everybody, God himself was undefiled. The personal and spiritual God of the Bible was lost in an indefinite pantheism.

It is altogether workable for a corresponding blunder (error) to be made with reference to the cross. Truth be told, such a blunder is very normal. That is the thing that happens when the cross of Jesus is given only the significance of the martyrdom of a good man. All things considered the centrality of the cross is diminished to that of the suffering of a good man and that as it were.

This technique for diminishing the criticalness of the significance of the incarnation and the cross of Jesus is the mistake of liberal Christianity and present day modern idealistic philosophy.

With reference to the extension of the thoughts of the incarnation and the cross to the people of God, there is a mistake likewise that belongs to the official or dictator kind of ecclesiology, alluded to above. The church is looked on as a supernaturally (divinely) authorized body. This divine commission (generally saw as having been given to the apostles and passed on by them to bishops or their successors) is viewed as having given the church the authority of Christ himself, with the goal that the church is viewed as the incarnation of Christ and consequently similar to his authoritative body in the world.

The authority of the church is the authority of Christ. Corresponding to this the eucharist is viewed as an actual sacrifice and as having divine adequacy for man's salvation. This makes the eucharist an extension or repetition of the value of the cross.

As over against these two kinds of view, the New Testament looks on restored humankind as an extension of the principle of the incarnation.

God abides in his people, however no one of them, nor every one of them together, is the incarnation of God in a similar sense that Jesus was, but his inhabiting in them is genuine and depends on God's incarnation in Christ.

In a comparable view the guideline of the cross is reproduced in Christ's people The cross is duplicated in them has not the saving adequacy for other people, that his cross has, however it is genuine and is basic for the extension of the cause for Christ in the world.

If God's people embody Christ, it is the Christ who died for sinners that they embody. In this manner they must embody the Spirit of the cross, in the event that they embody Christ.

Some Respects In Which The Christian Shares The Cross

Self-Denial

I. THE PRINCIPLE OF the cross is found in the Christian in that the Christian life is one of self-denial. Jesus said that one who should follow him should deny himself and take up his cross. To take up the cross is to die- to die to a narrow minded and common life (selfish and worldly life) and devote oneself to Christ and his service.

The self-denial that Jesus here instills isn't doing without this little delight or that. It is express and complete renunciation of self and self-authority. It is perceiving that one doesn't belong to himself, but that he has been purchased with a cost. It is surrendering oneself to Christ and his will as Christ surrendered himself to God and his will.

The possibility of self-denial here isn't that there is any an incentive in suffering's purpose. It isn't the kind of devotion that forces journeys on oneself, or pulls back from the world to live in forlorn self-examination and contemplation. Such piety as this may effortlessly turn into a types of

Dr. John Thomas Wylie

greedy that is the exact inverse of the spirit of the cross. The spirit of the cross is to offer oneself to God and others.

Such piety as we here talk about is simple self-repression. Self-repression isn't Christian self-denial. A real existence of Christian self-denial implies that one loses self in the service of Christ and one's fellows.

Evangelistic And Missionary Activity

2. THE SPIRIT OF the cross communicates in the evangelistic and missionary dynamic of the Christian life. A few people look on evangelistic or missionary action with respect to Christians as a types of contemptible proselyting or as some pugilistic religionist attempting to put his thoughts over on another person.

Such an understanding shows, that one holding it has an exceptionally shallow perspective of what Christianity implies in human life. Some of the time Christians are blamed for their missionary activity and are informed that they have no right to attempt to impose their religion on another person. In any case, the New Testament says that the gospel is uplifting news. One wants to advise, one will tell, uplifting news. He can't smother it.

Jesus died to bring to men in saving power the uplifting news of the love of God. Evangelists and missionaries around world today are giving their lives to bring to men in the darkness of wrongdoing (sin) the uplifting news of salvation through faith in his name. Men like Saul of Tarsus, William Carey, and a large number of others before and in the present, have yielded all the world tallies worth to carry to others the uplifting news of Christ and his cross.

Spreading the gospel is in every case expensive business. One can't generally do anything worth while at it except if he offers himself to it in the spirit of the cross. He should subordinate all else to Christ and his work. He should crucify self and natural aspiration. Truth be told that ought to be the spirit of every Christian and must be if his life counts for much the service of Christ.

We get a perspective of what broadening the gospel costs if we note the language of Paul in Romans 9:1-2. He says that he has extraordinary distress and constant torment in his heart. He could even wish himself accursed from Christ for his brethren, his kinsmen in the flesh, his

Dr. John Thomas Wylie

Israelitish brethren. Here is the spirit of the cross, and that was what sent Paul out over land and sea to tell men regarding the love of God in Christ. Present day Christianity has minimal missionary power in it on the grounds that has little of the passion of the cross.

This is one indictment that can be brought against current Unitarianism. It has almost no missionary or evangelistic dynamic in it. It might do for swivel seat teachers of religious philosophy who conjecture on the "issues" of religious theology.

But when such inquiries as the incarnation and cross of Christ turn out to be simply "issues" to theorize about instead of elements in Christian living, they are never again what they are in the New Testament. In the New Testament they are dynamic actualities and factors throughout everyday life, not just something about which impartially to theorize.

Intercessory Prayer

3. ONE PHASE OF the Christian life that is an outflow of the spirit of the cross is intercessory

prayer. By intercessory prayer we mean supplication in which we precede God for the benefit of another. It is supplication (prayer) in which we look for the blessing of God for the benefit of another person. It might look for the salvation of a lost soul, or looking for God's power on a Christian laborer, or something other than what's expected from both of these. Regardless, we are intercessors if we acquire God's blessing for another. We have various occurrences of such interventions in the Bible.

All such intercession is costly in a spiritual way. Maybe this is one reason Christians do as such little of it. It cost time, thought, exertion, vitality. It looks through one's heart and sanitizes his life.

It communicates the spirit of the cross in that it reveals an unselfish concern for the welfare of another. One's petitions for himself might be narrow minded, selfish, notwithstanding even when he supplicates for spiritual blessings. One isn't so prone to be narrow minded or selfish in petitioning God for a blessing on another person.

The cross is the immediate and total opposite of the spirit of self-centeredness. Intercessory prayer will create and will develop to expression this spirit in the Christian's life, and as the spirit is produced in his life he will have power in intercession.

In Exodus 19:6, Jehovah says that Israel is to be a kingdom of priests for him. We discover an articulation like this multiple times in the book of Revelation. John says that God made us to be a kingdom, even priests, unto the God and Father of Christ (Rev. 1:6). Maybe the thought in this impossible to miss expression is that, as God gets spiritual sovereignty over us, he utilizes us to mediate his power to other people.

God works through us. As we take part in intercessory prayer, we are not working against God. We are working with him against the sin and insidiousness, evil of the world. We are helping him to extend the victory of the cross in the lives of men around us.

Overcoming Evil With Good

4. SOMEWHERE ELSE WHERE it is very obvious that the Christian life is a reproducttion of the spirit of the cross is in the Christian method of defeating evil. The method for the world is to

conquer malicious with malicious or evil with evil. It is the law of striking back. We discover this law of striking back (retaliation) embodied in the Mosaic enactment of the Old Testament (Exod. 21:23,24; Lev. 24:19 ff.; Deut. 19:16-21).

It is to be noted, notwithstanding, that it isn't emdorsed in the Old Testament as something to be rehearsed or practiced between people accordingly. It is somewhat a guideline encapsulated to a constrained degree in common law. For the purposes behind civil government, at any rate in specific phases of moral and civic improvement, such a procedure is legitimate. It is a need. Power (force) should now and then be met with force.

That is valid in the dealings of society with criminal components. It is by all accounts essential, in any event as things presently seem to be, in the dealings of countries with worldwide rascals. Maybe this is one of the places where, as Paul says, the civil authority does bear the sword in vain (Rom. 13:1-4). Paul shows that civil government is ordained of God and is advocated in the utilization of force to achieve its closures.

The New Testament unmistakenly forbids a Christian to show the spirit of retaliation in

Dr. John Thomas Wylie

managing his fellow man. Jesus teaches rather than this (turn the other cheek) to accept punishment silently, go the second mile, and provide for the one that asks (Matt. 5:38 ff.). It appears to be not really important to state that Jesus isn't making up a standard book by which the Christian is to govern his conduct.

He is instilling a spirit a spirit which he himself displayed in his life. Nor was Jesus planning laws to oversee the state in connection to offenders, or society in connection to homeless people and destitution, or countries in connection to worldwide criminals. If we could ask him about these things, he likely would state: "Man, who made me a financial expert or a lawgiver over you?"

But he was attempting to ingrain a specific spirit into his disciples- a spirit they should show in all relations throughout everyday life. That spirit has done much for human culture and is bound to accomplish more later on.

In instructing them subsequently to act, Jesus referred to the case of the Heavenly Father (Matt. 5:43 ff.). God regards all men, good and terrible. We are not to regard those just who regard us.

After the case of the Heavenly Father, we are to do good to all men, even where they abuse us and aggrieve us. At the point when the Christian is aggrieved and abused, he has an uncommon chance to show the Spirit of God in relation to other men.

Paul demonstrates a similar spirit in Romans 12:119-21. Rather than getting revenge on our adversary, we are to do good to him. Leave the matter of getting revenge (vengeance) to God. He holds that privilege to himself. We are to try to beat evil with good.

In the event that anyone should demand that the good is feeble to defeat evil, the appropriate response is that good is the only thing that can beat evil. Detestable powers may counter each other, however, evil can not overcome evil. The only way that evil can be defeated is to transform the sinner into a holy person. So far as physical power (force) is concerned, it might be utilized or overruled to good closures, however physical force all things considered can't improve man.

Shouldn't something be said about the those who won't be transformed into the good? Does the technique for God's goodness or grace imply that the individuals who won't be changed are to be left to work their evil will in God's world? This would be a bogus derivation. Wicked men, sinful men who won't respect God's grace are not left allowed to work their malicious, evil designs in God's universe.

The universe is made to the point that those with evil designs rout their own closures. Underhandedness, sinfulness, evil is foolish. The Bible from beginning to end bears witness to thius fact. The man who burrows a pit for another falls into it himself (Psalm 7:15,16). The evil man who takes a sword against others will die by his very own sword (Psalm 37:15). This reality (that evil is foolishly self-defeating) isn't constantly clear immediately, however in time it will faultlessly prove true.

The man who conceives that he can disregard or oppose God, ridicule the laws of morality, seek after his very own egotistical closures and be happy will positively come to hopelessness. He will find that the whole universe, including his own inward nature, is against him in such an endeavor. Particularly is it true that the man who detests God's grace and won't have his mercy will find that the supremacy of the everlasting God was enveloped with the good of God that he cannot and that it bounce back on him to his doom or destruction.

The Cross And Blessedness

THE QUESTION EMERGES HERE. How is this thought of sharing the cross identified with the Christian's joy or blessedness? Here we please one of the extraordinary Catch 22s of the Christian life. One discovers his bliss (maybe better, blessedness) by sharing the cross.

Jesus express this conundrum in the Beatitudes by saying that the individuals who grieve are glad (or favored, blessed) (Matt. 5:4). In the passages previously referred to, we discover that one spares his life by losing it; one dies to live. It involves experience that they are simply the most joyful Christians who give completely to God in the service of others.

The Son of man came, not to be served, however to serve, and to give his life a ransom for many (Mark 10:45). Satisfaction isn't found in this world by staying away from duty and offering oneself to an actual existence of straightforwardness and extravagance. Narrow-mindedness (selfishness) dependably prompts wretchedness. Jesus for the joy that was set before him, persevered through the cross, loathing the disgrace (Heb. 12:2). He discovered his joy by persevering through the cross, not by sidestepping it. So should we.

Scholars and theologians once held, maybe some do yet, that God was impossible. They held that he couldn't suffer and be a righteous God, as well. This was an odd position for individuals to hold, the image of whose religion was a cross. The cross represents what it cost God to save us. He discovers his blessedness in blessing others, notwithstanding when blessing them implies a cross.

Any man will find that a religion without a cross at its center is a religion without authentic euphoria and harmony. The cross causes us to comprehend God, to decipher the universe, to locate the true importance of life. All the major inclinations of the ethical universe meet in the cross of Christ.

We won't seek after further, as of now, the possibility that the Christian offers and communicates the spirit of the cross. We trust we have said enough to make the point obvious.

Bibliography

Anselm, St. McCormick, R. D. (1903, 2005) Cur Deus Homo. Fort Worth, TX.: Chicago, Ill.: Canterbury, UK.: RDMC Publishing, The Open Court/Publishing Company

Augustine And boulding (1997) The Confessions. Hyde Park, NY.: New York City Press, Augustinian Heritage Institute

Boyce, J. P. (2006) The Abstract Of Systematic Theology. Bellingham, WA.: Founders Press, Faithlife, American Baptist

Burton, E. D. W., Powis, J. M., Smith, G. B. (1909) Biblical Ideas Of Atonement: Their History And Significance. Chicago, Ill.: University Of Chicago Press, Nubu Press Conner, W. T. (1936) Revelation And God. Nashville, TN.: Broadman Press

Edward, B. P. (1914, 2009) Book I Of St. Augustine. Canterbury, UK.: Evnity Publishing

Fairbairn, A. M. (1923, 1962, 2017) Philosophy Of The Christian Religion. Toronto, CA.:

University Of Toronto, Forgotten Books, BiblioLife, LLC

Garvie, A. E. (1925) The Christian Doctrine Of The Godhead. London, ENG.: Hodder & Stoughton

Mullina, E. Y. (1954-59, 1974) The Christian Religion In It's Doctrinal Expression (Classic Reprint). King Of Prussia, PA.: Baltimore, MD.: Mishawaka, IN.: Palala Press, Forgotten Books, Judson Press, Better World Books

Stevens, G. B. (1982, 2006) Pauline Theology – The Study Of The Origin And Correlation Of Doctrinal Teaching Of Paul. Yale University, USA.: Kessinger Publishing

Strong, A. H. (2009, 2016) Systematic Theology. King Of Prussia, PA.: Wentworth, NH.: Wentworth Press, Judson Press

The Holy Bible (1964) Authorized King James Version. Chicago, Ill.: J. G. Ferguson

The Holy Bible (1982) New International Version. Grand Rapids, MI.: Thomas Nelson Inc. (Used By Permission)

The Holy Bible (1953) The Revised Standard Version. Nashville, TN.: Thomas Nelson & Sons (Used By Permission)

The Holy Bible (1901) The American Standard Version. Nashville, TN.: Thomas Nelson (Used By Permission)

The Holy Bible (1959) The Berkeley Version. Grand Rapids, MI.: Zondervan (Used By Permission)

The New Testament In Language Of The People (1937, 1949) Chicago, Ill.: Charles B. Williams, Bruce Humphries, Inc, Moody Bible Institute (Used By Permission)

Printed in the United States
By Bookmasters